18.25

FASHION FOR DISABLED PEOPLE

FASHION FOR DISABLED PEOPLE

Nellie Thornton

B.T. Batsford Ltd
London

ISBN 0 7134 6129 2

Typeset by Servis Filmsetting Ltd, Manchester
and printed by
Butler and Tanner, Frome, Somerset

for the publishers
B.T. Batsford Ltd
4 Fitzhardinge Street
London W1H 0AH

CONTENTS

Acknowledgements

I would like to thank Hazel Howard, Sheila Wright and Charlene Stead for their invaluable assistance in the writing of this book; Jenny Valentine for her illustrations; Adrian Bampton for the photographs; Margaret, Anne, Caroline, Claire, Samantha, Zubaida, Iris, Maureen and Rosemary for modelling; the staff of Fashion Services for the Disabled Workshop for their help.

LIST OF ILLUSTRATIONS

INTRODUCTION

I wonder if you have ever stopped to think why we wear clothes? The reasons that may spring to mind are attraction, decency, warmth, protection and, most importantly, a sense of belonging. All these factors are particularly relevant when applied to people with disabilities.

We all wear clothes to make us look more attractive, or to attract attention to ourselves when we have a statement to make. A disabled person attracts attention anyway. Unfortunately many people see the disability first and the person second. We need to make sure that attention is drawn to his or her good points and away from the disability. As one mum who had just designed and made a dress for her Downs Syndrome daughter said, 'It's good to know that people are looking at my little girl because she looks nice now, not because she's disabled.'

A feeling of belonging is important to all of us. We like to know we are a recognized part of a society, club or group and, even more important, that we are accepted by the community at large. Disabled teenagers want to be a part of the fashion scene and wear what their able-bodied peers are wearing, not sit on the side-lines and watch fashion pass them by. Disabled men and women only ask to be able to look like everyone else, while older people may need to feel 'respectable'. If able-bodied people don't have the right clothes for the occasion, they go out and buy something, make something, or even borrow something. Disabled people don't have that sort of choice. They cannot buy clothing that hangs and fits correctly and, in many cases, are too ashamed to go out in what they have, so they stay at home.

Decency involves dressing in a manner which is socially acceptable to the company we keep and the country and times in which we live. Disabled people may find that, because they have limited use in their hands, manoeuvering garments for dressing or toileting is time-consuming, often *too* time-consuming. Consequently pants, bras or girdles remain half on or are left off entirely, which causes embarrassment and distress. Body shape can be the cause of skirts riding up to expose urine bags, or half pulled-up stockings, and it can also create gaping necklines which reveal all. In many cases disabled people become housebound, not because they are unable to move but because they feel untidy, different, socially unacceptable in the clothing they are able to wear. Unfortunately this can also affect the lifestyle of the partner.

Warmth, for most of us, means dressing to suit the temperature or our surroundings or the time of year. Disabled people with paralysis or poor circulation can be constantly cold. As warmth is created by air being trapped between layers of fabric or fibres, we have always been told to wear a number of garments to keep warm. This is tiring from the point of view of getting dressed, increases the weight of clothing and restricts movement. Special lightweight fibres and fabrics (which give the required warmth) are manufactured for sporting activities and these are of great value for people with a warmth problem. Other people, like amputees or with thalidomide-type problems, tend to get too hot, and their need is for fabrics which are cool and absorbent.

Protection is mainly related to the work we do. We may need to wear gloves, aprons, helmets, fireproof or waterproof clothing. We also wear light-coloured clothing to reflect the sun's rays and save us from getting too hot or burnt by the sun. Disabled people need to consider the extra wear and tear on clothing caused by difficulties in getting dressed and by appliances. Sleeve and skirt lengths and widths need to be considered for people using wheelchairs, crutches or sticks. Protection is needed for those who have little or no control of mouth muscles and tend to dribble, otherwise their upper clothing will be constantly wet, which often leads to chest infections. Delicate skin needs protection from rubbing or pressure caused by rough seams or bulky fastenings. Suitable garments are needed for incontinence problems, helmets may be needed for some people who have epilepsy, and in a few cases of mental illness, clothing is needed to protect the person from injuring him- or herself.

This book is not exclusively a book on fashion, dressmaking, or pattern making, though all these items are included. The following chapters highlight the clothing problems which all of us have to some degree but which are magnified greatly for disabled people, offer ideas and solutions related to style, colour and fabric choice, and suggest alterations to ready-made garments and to bought patterns. I would like to feel that everyone reading this book will benefit from a further insight into the way we dress, but I aim the book specifically towards the following groups of people, without whose help we cannot achieve our aim to improve the self-image and lifestyle of people with a disability.

People working in the field of clothing design, pattern cutting, and fabric and garment construction will perhaps get an insight into the clothing problems of disabled people and bear them in mind when designing fabrics and clothing. Many garments could be designed to be acceptable to both able-bodied and disabled people, which would solve many problems. A disabled person wants to shop where everyone else shops, though there will always be some who need personally designed clothing and specialist fabrics.

Home dressmakers will get a deeper understanding of the difficulties involved in making clothes for disabled people and the possible ways of overcoming them. It is so easy to see a person as a 'shape problem' but have no idea what other difficulties there are because we don't like asking personal questions. Workshops making clothing to order are rather thin on the ground in places and your expertise is desperately needed.

Those working with and caring for people with a disability will find solutions which make shopping and dressing a happy occasion rather than a wearisome chore. You might find that you are saying, 'That's simple, why didn't I think of that', and you will go on to solve many other problems without our help.

Disabled people will become more involved in the choosing, designing and making of their clothes and will enjoy the satisfaction and confidence they gain from it. They have the problems, and only with their help can we hope to solve them.

Let us all work together to give disabled people the choice of clothing that the able-bodied have enjoyed for years. Let us give them confidence, restore their dignity, and make them feel a very real part of the community. We must remember that you can only design *with* a disabled person, not *for* them, only *advise* not *insist*. If disabled people are going to enjoy wearing their clothes, the final choice must rest with them.

1 THE IMPORTANCE OF FASHION

Clothes have a much greater effect on our lives than many of us realize. Whether we 'wear what we can get into' and stay at home, or make an effort to look good and live life to the full depends on each one of us. Looking good isn't always something that happens naturally; it's something we usually have to work at. The following rhyme appeared in a magazine many years ago.

I wonder why, with wardrobe large
    and stuffed for all to see,
With garments bright and garments dull,
    There's often nothing 'me'.

Every woman has, at some time, taken a dress out of the wardrobe, put it on, looked at herself in the mirror, and taken it off again. It wasn't right. It fitted beautifully, but it wasn't 'her'. Perhaps it didn't suit her mood, or the occasion, or maybe it didn't flatter her figure or suit her colouring. We can see garments on friends and neighbours, on models in the shops and in mail order catalogues and they look wonderful, but it doesn't follow that the same style and colour is going to look wonderful on us. We are all individuals with different shapes, colourings, personalities and lifestyles, and we need to find out what suits us. The way we dress tells people a lot about us, and also what we want them to know about us.

In a crowd you can pick out the shy person or the person who likes to be noticed, the one who worries about the image she portrays or the one who couldn't care less, the nervous type who wears fussy clothes and lots of jewellery or the super-efficient (Fig. 1). We are often judged by our appearance when applying for a job or meeting people for the first time, and if our choice of

1 Clothes talk

clothing does not work for us we can give a totally wrong impression. It is important for us to feel that the clothes we are wearing are suited to the occasion. From this knowledge we gain confidence in ourselves.

James was a young man of small stature. He was going for an interview for a job and felt he should wear a suit for this important occasion. He couldn't buy one to fit him so he decided to make one. He was very proud, not only of the image he presented, but of the fact that he could say at the interview, that he had made it himself. This was no small achievement! It gave him tremendous confidence and he got the job. In appearance he presented himself as a smart young man. He also showed that he was prepared to work much harder than most of us to produce that image, that he was a neat worker and paid attention to detail, and that he had confidence in himself and his abilities.

We all need to look good, but it is particularly important for a disabled person. Wheelchairs, crutches and sticks are things that attract attention, as do asymmetrical shapes. We have to fade these into insignificance and make people see the personality handling the appliance or living within the shape. Appliances are useful, and our shapes we have to learn to live with, but we must not let them take over our lives. It's the person that is important, and it's the person who is so often ignored. Everyone has something about them that is beautiful, and it's this that we want everyone else to see. By good use of style and colour and eye-catching accessories we can make people look wherever we want them to look, and not see the disability. A middle-aged lady I once met had bright green hair. She told me that she had shocking legs but nobody ever noticed them. She had the right idea, though there is no need to be quite so drastic!

The knowledge that we look good boosts our morale, and gives confidence. Self-confidence leads us to try new things, go to new places, meet new people. Suddenly life has a real purpose. No one is useless. We all have something to give. If we look untidy and feel depressed when we see ourselves in a mirror we shall also have a depressing effect on the people who live and work with us. But if we present a good image, everyone is happy.

Many disabled people cannot buy the clothing they would like to wear because of the varying problems they have. How do you project a favourable image of yourself when you literally have to wear what you can get into? How can you feel you 'belong' when what is available to the able-bodied is not available to you? A lot depends on the fashion of the moment. When styles are baggy buying is easier, but when fitted garments are the fashion of the day shopping becomes much more difficult for a person with a disability.

Always take your measurements and a tape measure with you when you go shopping. If there are suitable facilities for trying on garments in the shop and you have help with you, then this is advisable. Failing that, don't be afraid to lay the garment on the counter to check width measurements, and fold out parts of the garment to give yourself the correct lengths. When you have shortened your garment in the required areas does it still look good? It is better to know now than be disappointed when the necessary alterations have been made.

Even if you never seem to find anything that is 'really you' and you get very disheartened, read on. Designing and making your own clothing, or being involved in the process, can be very satisfying, less expensive, and lots of fun. You may not be able to do everything yourself, but a group of disabled people should each be able to manage a different process. For example, you may have good ideas but are unable to use your hands, so you talk and let someone else draw. You may not be able to use your legs and can only use one arm. Let someone else drive the machine while you guide the fabric. Problems are never so bad when you share them.

2 A DESIGNER'S TOOLS: COLOUR AND LINE

Over the years, fashion silhouettes have changed our body shape – or appeared to. We have had A-lines, tents, sacks, tubes, peg tops, shapes that hide the basic body shape completely, and some that reveal all. By the clever use of colour, line and fabric, designers have made the body appear to be a different shape to the one it actually is (Fig. 2). People with a disability find they have problems with proportion, size and shape. By using the same 'tools' as the designers, we can make the body appear to be in proportion, and look thinner, wider, longer or shorter to play down the problem areas.

When designing anything, proportion, balance, rhythm and detail are used to give a pleasing effect. Proportion is to do with the way the garment is divided either by style lines or colour. This division can make the top half of the body appear longer or shorter, and it is important that we do not shorten an already foreshortened area by the style we choose. Balance is related to the interest in a garment. It can be symmetrical, like a shirt-waisted style or a double-breasted garment, or asymmetrical, where the interest is more to one side, as in a wrap-over garment, or where there is a diagonal division. Rhythm is created when the eye can move smoothly over the garment and is not jumping from one point of interest to another. The points of interest are the details, for instance buttons, bows, ruffles, or top-stitching. These must also be in proportion to the rest of the garment and to figure size and shape.

Colour

Colour is the first thing we notice about people's clothes. We refer to a blue coat or a red dress rather than to a swing-back or princess line. Colour affects our lives and our moods. Some colours are dull, some cheerful, some subtle, some bold, some warm, some cool, and we choose colours to suit our moods and the occasion. Unfortunately the colours we like don't always like us. If a colour you are particularly fond of does not suit you, it is best to restrict it to skirts or trousers. It is the colour next to our faces that is important. Because of this, our personal colouring needs to be taken into account. Women can use make-up to adjust their facial colouring to complement a colour that might otherwise appear too bold or too pale.

Bernat Klein, in his book *An Eye for Colour*, relates colours that suit you to the colours in your eyes. If you look into your eyes in a mirror you will see that there are four or five different colours there. All these colours will suit you, and can be lightened or darkened to complement your complexion and hair colouring. The colours can be mixed together to give softer, subtle tones, and contrasts to these can be used for accessories, or on their own. Greys and beiges, in which there is a hint of one of your original eye colours, are the neutrals for you.

A more modern method is skin analysis, and there are analysts around the country who would be happy to advise and give you a

2 Fashion thro' the ages

personal colour chart. They base their colours on the undertone of the skin, and eye and hair colouring, and categorize you into a spring, summer, autumn or winter person. Spring people have a gold undertone and a clear, bright complexion. They blush easily and are normally fair-haired with blue or green eyes. They can wear the clear colours of spring which are blues, turquoise, yellows and golds, warm pinks and creamy whites. Summer people have a blue undertone but their skin colouring has pink in it. Hair can be anything from blond to dark brown, eye colourings vary. They can wear the softer,

hazy colours of summer. Soft whites, and colours with blue in them are found on the cool side of the colour chart. Autumn people have golden undertones and often have freckles. Hair is red or golden, eyes brown or green. For them the colours of autumn leaves, soft white and blue. Winter people have a blue undertone and a darker complexion, dark hair and dark eyes. They can wear dramatic, bold colours and are the only group that can carry pure white.

Doris Pooser, in her book *Always in Style*, has good colour charts and goes into the analysis in detail. Mary Quant, in *Colour by Quant*, agrees that people have either blue or

3 Colour circle

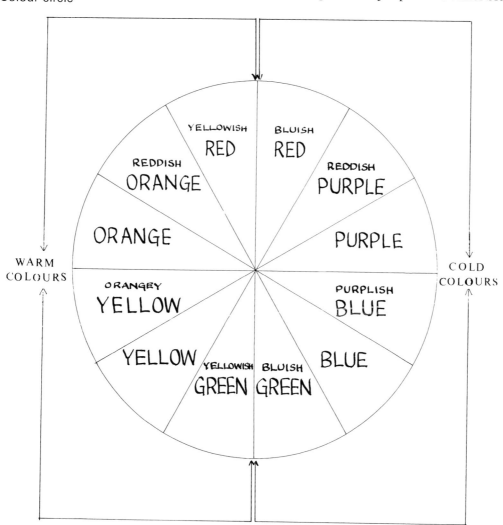

yellow undertones, the blues looking best in cooler colours, the yellows in warmer ones. But she also says, 'If you fancy a colour, don't fight it. Adjust your make-up, put on a bold front, and wear what you like with confidence.' There are people with that kind of confidence who could and would follow Mary Quant's advice, but there are others, lacking in confidence, who need the guidance of Doris Pooser or Bernat Klein. They need to follow the rules until they have the confidence to experiment and bend or break them. Different analysts have different ideas. It is advisable to look at a number of books, and choose the one which seems right for you.

When buying fabrics or garments remember that colours look different under striplighting to how they appear in daylight. If the garment is for evening-wear artificial light is fine, but if it is for day-wear check the colours in the shop doorway – with permission, of course! Always drape the fabric over your shoulders or hold dresses, blouses, jumpers, shirts or jackets next to your face in front of a mirror. Does the colour make you look tired or ill, does it overpower you, or does it make you look good and feel good? If you don't have faith in your own decisions, make sure you have someone with you whose judgement you trust. Don't be talked into something if you have doubts. It's you that has to wear it.

The colour circle (Fig. 3)

Primary colours are red, yellow and blue. These can be mixed in different proportions to give a variety of colours, from red through violet to blue, through green to yellow, and yellow through orange to red. 'Warm' colours are from red with an orange tinge through orange and yellow to green with a yellow tinge, while 'cool' colours are from red with a purple tinge through violet and blue to green with a blue tinge. White or black can be added to give tints (with white), or shades (with black) of that colour. Col-

ours can be mixed together to give more subtle tones in the resultant mix; browns come into the warm colours and greys into the cool colours.

Colours diagonally opposite each other on the wheel are known as complementary contrasts, each one showing the other to its best advantage: for example, red with green. To be pleasantly effective, contrasts should be used in the same depth of colour. A true red, used with pale green (i.e. green with white added) is discordant, as would be yellow with pale violet, or orange with pale blue. Dark-toned colours are slimming because they absorb the light. For example, a dark-coloured top will play down your bust or chest size, while a dark skirt or trousers will slim your hips.

4 Effect of vertical and horizontal lines

Line

Our eyes follow lines naturally from left to right and from top to bottom – as they do when we read, but they follow the horizontal line more readily than the vertical. A straight line is followed quickly by the eye, and this makes it appear severe. A curve is followed more slowly and gives a softer effect. Lines create illusions, and these can be used to good effect when designing clothes, particularly for people with a disability. Vertical lines lead the eye up and down, giving an impression of height. Horizontal lines lead the eye across, emphasizing width (Fig. 4). Fabric patterns often have a line and direction of their own which can be stronger than the style lines. Be careful not to choose styles with lines going round your widest part as this will make it appear even wider (Figs. 5 and 6)! A single line is more effective than repeated lines, because in the first instance the eye follows the line quickly; with a number of lines the eye must move sideways from one to the other, and this breaks the effect (Fig. 7).

(a)   (b)   (c)

a & b emphasize a large bust   *c takes the eye to the hipline*

5 Correct use of line for large bust

(a)　　　　　　(b)　　　　　　(c)

a emphasizes large hips　　　*b & c take the eye upwards*

6 Correct use of line for large hips

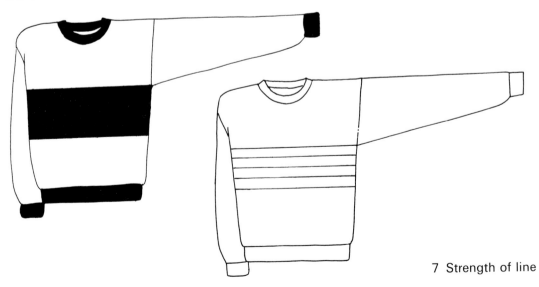

7 Strength of line

8 Effect of stripes

9 Stripes on an asymmetrical figure

Fig. 8 shows how stripes can be used to lengthen or shorten areas and the effects they can have. An unbroken silhouette gives height. Be careful not to use striped or checked fabrics on the straight of the fabric if the body is asymmetrical, as they will emphasize figure faults (Fig. 9).

A line above the waist will appear to lengthen the lower half of the body, while a line below the waist will appear to lengthen the top half of the body. If you need to keep your skirt at a certain length, to keep up with fashion and to appear to change its length you can alter instead the length of your jackets, jumpers or cardigans. A shorter jacket will make your skirt look longer, a long jacket will give the illusion of a shorter skirt. For men, a shorter jacket will make the legs appear longer, while a longer jacket will shorten the legs (Fig. 10).

Short diagonal lines lead the eye from side to side and have a broadening effect, while long diagonals, from top to bottom, make

10 Proportion

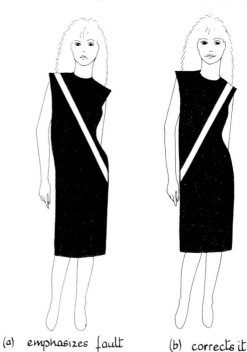

DIAGONALS ARE EFFECTIVE,
BUT HAVE WE GOT THE RIGHT EFFECT?

(a) *emphasizes* fault   (b) *corrects it*

11 Effect of diagonals

12 Use of diagonals

the body appear shorter (Fig. 11). They can be useful in 'lifting' a low shoulder, or in helping to balance a scoliosis (Fig. 12).

Necklines

Necklines draw attention to the face and are important shaping lines. People with short necks should avoid wearing garments with turtle or polo necklines, ruffles or high collars as these cover up part of the neck and make it appear even shorter. Conversely, V-shaped, square, or U-shaped necklines add

13 Suitable collars for a short neck

23

14 Camouflaging necklines

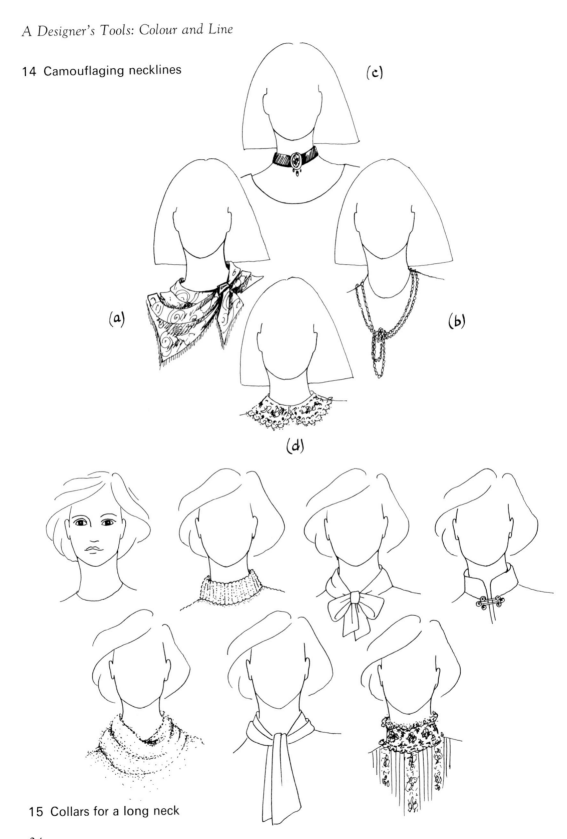

(c)

(a)

(b)

(d)

15 Collars for a long neck

length to the neck (Fig. 13). If, for some reason, you need to wear a high neckline, necklaces and loosely tied scarves can help lead the eye downwards and detract from the shortening effect. For men, an open-necked shirt lengthens the neck, but if preference or convention demand a buttoned collar a conventional tie will take the eye downwards anyway (Figs. 14a and 14b).

High necklines are for people with longer necks – bows, cowls, mandarin and polo-type collars appear to shorten the neck (Fig. 15). Should you wish to wear a low neck for evenings, a choker necklace will break the line (Fig. 14c). In the same way, a bow tie or cravat will shorten the neckline for men. Detail draws attention, and should be used to attract attention to the wearer's good points and away from the disability. Pretty collars draw the eye to the face (Fig. 14d), as do bows, necklaces and brooches, especially in contrasting colours.

Style lines

We all know what we like when we browse around the shops or through catalogues, but do we know what will really suit us? There are a number of good books that deal with self-image and colour. They are well worth reading, but they do not always offer the same advice. Some suggest we should follow the lines of our body and wear either straight, tailored clothes or curvy, softer-styled clothing, while others feel that we should camouflage our bodies to suggest shapes that we are not. In fact, both these ideas are used when designing for difficult body shapes. At Fashion Services for the Disabled we aim to make people appear to be in proportion and to play down faults, but we also want to bring out the personality of the person, and this is reflected in their choice of garments.

We should start by knowing the shape of our bodies. The easy way to do this is to have a photograph taken wearing something reasonably fitted. Underwear is ideal, but fail-

ing that, a tailored blouse or shirt with trousers is acceptable, provided that the waistline is visible. This photograph can be enlarged on a photocopier to enable you to trace round the outline (Fig. 16).

16 Traced figure with scoliosis

Look through magazines and catalogues and choose styles that appeal to you. Draw them on to your shape, and see what they do for you. It may help to ask yourself some questions like the following:

1 Can you take a natural waistline? Does it need to move up or down to put the body in proportion? Or are you better without a waistline at all?
2 Do your shoulders need width, which can be gained by gathered or pleated sleeve-heads or a padded raglan sleeve?
3 Is the neckline attractive?

25

4 Do you need to look longer, and would a front opening give that line down, and make the garment easier to manage?
5 Is your attention drawn to the right places?
6 Is the balance right when the length of the jacket, top, skirt or trousers is drawn where you want it?

The answers to these questions will help you to make a collection of shapes that look good on you and that you like. This will guide your choice when you go shopping either for patterns or garments and will help you avoid disappointment.

Fig. 17a shows what would happen to a waisted garment on our traced figure with a scoliosis. The dotted line on Fig. 17b shows the sort of garment line we need to help lift the shoulder and straighten the body. Figs. 18a, 18b and 18c show suitable styles, all different, but all of which give us a means of correcting the hang of the garment, draw attention away from the actual waistline and give a line which camouflages the scoliosis.

17a Waisted dress

17b Required hang

18a Suitable styles for scoliosis

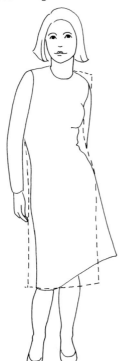

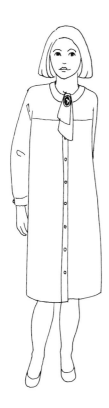

18b

18c

19 Spina bifida

Let us take another example of a different body shape: a young woman with spina bifida who walks with the aid of sticks (Fig. 19). Her arms are short, and often jumper sleeves are too long, creating wrinkles. If her hips are large and the jumper is too tight fitting, the bottom of the jumper will ride up, adding to the problem. Trousers emphasize the body shape and are often too long, but don't get in the way of sticks. Fig. 20a shows a longer, looser jumper with shorter trousers. The necklace adds length. Figs. 20b and 20c show jacket styles with a lengthening effect which camouflage the hips and lengthen the neck. Fig. 20d shows a day dress. It gives room for movement to walk with sticks. A contrasting collar draws attention to the face, and a button-through fastening adds height. The skirt width is kept to a minimum. Fig. 20e shows pretty evening co-

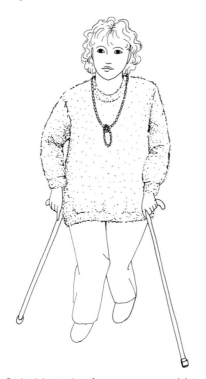

20c

20a Suitable styles for someone with spina
     bifida

20b

20d

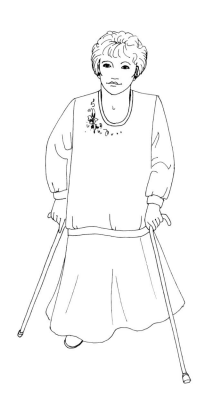

20e

fabric like mohair, or a loosely woven tweed or bouclé. Smooth, tightly woven fabrics give straight lines, while textured fabrics give a softer line, but they also add bulk.

Finally, the best method of deciding what fabrics, prints and trimming detail suits you is to look at your bone structure, particularly in your face. If you are small boned choose delicate detail. Fabrics should be fine, prints small and buttons may be distinctive but should be small. Large buttons, heavy trim and bulky fabrics would be too overpowering. People with a bigger bone structure can carry the heavier fabrics, larger prints, bigger buttons and bold trim. But no matter what your bone structure is like, if one part of your body is disproportionally large it is best to avoid distinctive trimming details of any kind in that area (Fig. 21).

ordinates which lengthen the neck and use embroidery to draw attention to the face. The blouson top comes below hip level, and the skirt is only slightly flared.

Two other factors contribute to style lines: the pattern and texture of the fabric. Prints should be in proportion to the figure size. As a general rule, small prints are suitable for small people, larger prints for larger people, and for the very large a pattern in tones of the same colour, or no pattern at all. Doris Pooser suggests that if you have a square or oblong face you should look for geometric prints, but if your face is round or oval softer lines and florals are more likely to flatter. Fabric texture is also important. You cannot create a straight line with a hairy

WHY DO I ALWAYS FANCY THE CLOTHES YOU SHOULD BE WEARING?

21 Cartoon on suitable trims for figure size

3 A DESIGNER'S TOOLS: FABRICS

In the last chapter we stressed the importance of meeting the clothing needs of the individual by getting the fit right and by producing or buying a garment in an attractive style and colour. For a disabled person comfort and easy access to appliances must also be considered, and fastenings must be of a kind suited to the independence of the wearer. Fabrics play a vital role in solving these problems, ensuring comfort and making dressing easier. The wrong choice of fabric can create further problems. How easy it is to be attracted to a fabric by its design and colour and ignore the fibre content. Laundering also needs to be considered, as the care of the garment is limited by the ability of the wearer and by the facilities available.

Fibres Most Commonly Used in Fabrics for Clothes

FIBRES

NATURAL		MAN-MADE	
Animal	**Vegetable**	**Regenerated Cellulose**	**Synthetic**
Wool			Polyamide (nylon)
Alpaca			Polyester
Llama	Cotton	Viscose	Acrylic
Angora	Flax (linen)	Acetate	Modacrylic
Camel } Staple	Flax (linen) }	Triacetate	Elastofibre (Elastane)
Vicuna	Ramie		Chlorofibre (Thermolactyl)
Mohair			
Cashmere			
Silk	Filament		

NOTES

Staple — All natural fibres, with the exception of silk, are restricted in length. They range from cotton, which averages from 18 mm ($\frac{3}{4}$ in.) to 38 mm ($1\frac{1}{2}$ in.) long, to linen which can be up to 51 cm (20 in.) long. These are called staple fibres.

Filament — A filament fibre is one continuous length. Silk is the only natural filament fibre. Synthetic fibres are all produced as continuous filaments, but can be cut up to resemble natural fibres.

Regenerated Cellulose — Cellulose is a fibrous substance common to all forms of plant life. Wood pulp is most usually used in the production of fibres for textiles. It is dissolved into a viscose solution and extruded through a spinneret (similar to a watering-can rose) to form filament fibres when dried.

Synthetic — Synthetic fibres are manufactured chemically, usually from a petroleum derivative.

Fibre Properties

Fibre	Advantages	Disadvantages	Care
COTTON	Absorbent Cool Good strength but lightweight Good abrasion resistance Soft and smooth Blends well	Creases without special finish Poor drape Affected by perspiration	Washable Dry-cleanable Stands hot water, strong soaps and detergents Can shrink unless treated
LINEN	Absorbent Cool Strong Faster drying than cotton Blends well Better drape than cotton Smooth fibres do not collect dirt	Creases unless treated Low abrasion resistance Affected by perspiration	Washable Dry-cleanable Softness enhanced by repeated washings Can shrink, but less than cotton
RAMIE	A plant from S.E. Asia similar to flax and increasingly used as an alternative to linen and having similar properties		
SILK	Absorbent Warm Soft but strong Durable and resilient Blends well Good drape Does not attract dirt	Low abrasion resistance Low heat resistance Sunlight, perspiration and bleach damage fibres	Creases hang out Dry-cleanable Hand-washable Susceptible to water marks Iron damp, low temperature on wrong side Some shrinkage can occur
WOOL	Very absorbent Warm Durable Resilient Blends well Good drape	Low strength, particularly when wet Deterioration in strong sunlight Affected by perspiration	Some wools can be machine washed – check Dry-cleanable Hand-washable Can shrink
VISCOSE	Absorbent Warm Stronger than wool Anti-static Blends well Good drape	Poor abrasion resistance Limited resilience Limited elasticity Affected by perspiration	Washable with care Dry cleans well Sheds dirt Shrinks (spun more than filament) Weak when wet

MODAL	Properties as above, but developed to improve wet strength, washability, abrasion resistance and resilience		

ACETATE	Water-repellent
	Resilient
	Blends well
	Good drape
		Low absorbency
		Limited abrasion
		  resistance
		Low tensile
		  strength
		Limited elasticity
		Accumulates static
		Low wet strength
			Washable with care
			Dry-cleanable
			Quick drying
			Crease-resistant
			Can shrink
			Heat-sensitive

TRI-ACETATE	Modified form of acetate as above, but more robust than acetate, with improved elasticity		

POLYAMIDE
(NYLON)
	Very strong
	High abrasion
	  resistance
	Resilient
	Durable
	Drape dependent on
	  fabric construction
	Spun staple nylon –
	  good insulator
		Low absorbency
		Accumulates static
		Nylon staple pills
		  easily
			Washable
			Non-shrink
			Crease-resistant
			Quick drying
			Heat-sensitive

ACRYLIC	Warm
	Non-irritant
	Bulky fibre but
	  lightweight
	Resilient
	Durable
	Good elasticity
		Low absorbency
		Low abrasion
		  resistance
		Some fibre
		  constructions
		  pill badly
		Low wet strength
		Flammable
			Machine-washable
			Rapid drying
			Crease-resistant

MODACRYLIC	As above, but improved absorbency and wet strength and incorporating high flame resistance		

POLYESTER	Strong and resilient
	Warm to handle
	Cool in filament
	  form
	Bulked for insulation
	Blends well
		Low absorbency
		Pills in staple fibre
		  forms
		Low elasticity
		Accumulated static
			Washable
			Quick drying
			Oily stains difficult
			  to remove

ELASTANE	Strong
	Lighweight
	High elasticity
		Non-absorbent	Hand or machine
			  wash
			Drip- or tumble-
			  dry
			Damaged by
			  chlorine bleach

CHLOROFIBRE	Warm
	Lightweight
		Low absorbency
		Tendency to
		  yellow with age
		Accumulates static
		Melts and shrinks at
		  low temperatures
			Wash in lukewarm
			  water
			Do not tumble-dry
			  or use any
			  artificial heat
			  source

The preceding charts should help you choose your fabric. They show what fabrics are on the market and the properties each one possesses. We then give advice for different problem areas, and explain new and specialist fabrics in detail.

Warmth

There are many different types of disability and possibly the only generalization which can be made is the need for warm clothing. The majority of disabilities are immobilizing, and as it is activity which generates heat; when activity is reduced there is an increased susceptibility to cold. Very often poor circulation means a person feels the cold more intensely. Both warmth and activity help to improve circulation. Warm blood vessels dilate, making circulation more effective. Where there is little mobility, peripheral circulation can be poor so that hands and feet are constantly cold.

Of all the natural fibres, **wool** offers the most warmth. However, it is not the fibre itself which creates warmth, but rather the amount of air capable of being trapped within the fabric. The fibres of wool are structured in such a way as to hold each other apart and so create spaces for air. These pockets of air are warmed by the body and form an insulating layer. Several layers of thinner clothing are often advocated to create layers of trapped, insulating air. While this is quite an acceptable solution for able-bodied people, where dressing proves difficult one effective layer of fabric is more manageable.

The insulation offered by a fabric is in direct proportion to its thickness. Different constructions of yarn improve or reduce the amount of air trapped within a fabric. A thick, loosely woven fabric will consequently offer more warmth than a fine, closely woven yarn. In fact, wool need not always be associated with warmth. A fine woollen cloth, such as wool challis, pro-vided it is used in a loose-fitting style, can produce cool clothing.

Wool is not without its disadvantages, however. A woollen coat can be a heavy garment and can be very difficult to wear for anyone with restricted movement or painful joints. It could also make unaided dressing impossible. Under such circumstances, a quilted fabric might be the answer. These fabrics have a light-weight, synthetic filling, which imitates sheep's wool in its state prior to spinning, usually sandwiched between an outer shell fabric and an inner lining. Bulk, and hence insulation, is achieved without weight. These fabrics can vary widely in price, and it can sometimes be a false economy to buy at the cheaper end of the market because cheaper fillings can clog and compact with repeated washings, and therefore any insulation value is lost.

Acrylic is a synthetic fabric which can provide equal warmth to wool. Its major disadvantage is its flammability. It can burn explosively if it comes in contact with fire. Because of this danger it is banned from some hospitals and similar institutions. If clothing is stored communally a mass of acrylic garments can pose a considerable fire hazard.

Chlorofibre (thermolactyl) produces a fabric which, weight for weight, is as warm as any other, but it is a PVC fabric and needs careful washing, and garments made from this fibre can shrink drastically in a tumble-dryer. White garments also tend to take on a greyish hue quickly. Before choosing such a fabric washing arrangements need to be assessed. In all probability it would be inappropriate to select such garments for people living in an institutional setting.

Coolness

Although most disabled people require warm clothing, there are exceptions to this rule. Certain disabilities have the opposite effect. In many cases, amputees can experience constant overheating due to the body's thermostat failing to compensate for missing limbs. People with spinal injuries can often sweat excessively due to an inability to control their body temperatures. In such instances cool clothing is essential.

Cotton has the property of actively transporting heat away from the body and is therefore an ideal fabric for people who overheat. **Viscose** and **Modal**, made from a similar natural base fibre, are also cool. However, even when a fabric is inherently cool, certain kinds of construction, such as looped towelling or a brushed or napped surface, can increase the amount of air trapped within the fabric and consequently provide a degree of warmth. To be cool a fabric needs to be constructed from smooth filament yarns which are fine and loosely spun.

Wool and cotton are the two most commonly used natural fibres, but both have certain disadvantages. Wool needs careful washing and drying and is not very durable; 100 per cent cotton can take a long time to dry and it creases badly, making ironing difficult (see Fabric Care section). Perhaps the best way to overcome the disadvantages of wool and cotton is to blend them with other fibres. A 'blend fabric' is one which has been woven or knitted from yarn made by the blending of two or more fibres prior to the yarn being spun. A 'mixture fabric' is one where two or more different yarns are used during weaving or knitting (e.g. a nylon warp woven into a rayon or cotton weft). Both wool and cotton blend successfully with synthetic fibres, and this can greatly improve wear and washability. It is possible to add up to 25 per cent of a synthetic fibre in a blend without radically altering the beneficial properties of the natural fibre.

Absorbency and Moisture Transportation

People who constantly feel too warm and sweat freely need absorbent fabrics. Body braces and similar appliances can also cause sweating, and absorbency is needed to reduce the risk of sores from chaffing. **Viscose** and **Modal** are the only man-made fibres which are absorbent, because their base is regenerated cellulose, similar to cotton. All natural fibres are absorbent, and therefore preferable, but as discussed earlier, they can be slow to dry, which may mean a person will become cold and clammy. A blend with a small percentage of synthetic fibre may solve this difficulty.

There are occasions when a non-absorbent fabric is necessary. Fabrics made of **polypropylene** fibre have the useful property of allowing liquid to pass through without the fabric itself becoming wet. Thus the skin is kept dry. This can be particularly useful when dealing with problems like incontinence. Polypropylene is also permeable to air and so can prevent clamminess. It is more commonly used for items like nappy- or panty-liners, draw sheets and cushion or seat covers than it is for clothes.

If a disabled person wears a non-absorbent polyester fabric and sits on a non-absorbent PVC or similar wheelchair seat, and if that person has been sweating, the seat may become wet. This is because the moisture is not absorbed by the fabric but passes straight through to the seat. The name given to this process of transporting moisture is 'wicking'. Able-bodied people may experience a similar effect, but they will have the opportunity to move away, whereas a wheelchair user does not. Recently developed fabrics are helping to overcome this problem. They combine a natural fibre yarn and its absorbent properties with a synthetic yarn which is both non-absorbent and has the facility to 'wick' away moisture. They are made as two-layer, link-knitted fabrics. The inner yarn is a moisture-transporting polyamide or polyester, and the outer layer is of absorbent cotton or wool. As the inner layer allows body moisture through to the outer layer the skins remains dry. The outer absorbent layer spreads the moisture which allows it to evaporate quickly. So there is no cold clammy feeling, because the layer next to the skin remains dry.

Static

Synthetic, non-absorbent fibres are especially prone to static build-up because they are conductors of electricity. The build-up of static can cause several problems. It can be generated between clothing and seats, particularly if a disabled person wears a polyurethane body brace and sits on a PVC seat. If the person is insulated by rubber-soled shoes or wheelchair wheels the static charge will earth through anyone else who touches the disabled person and the other person will experience a slight electric shock.

Static build-up is also increased in a dry atmosphere, which often exists in hospitals and residential homes, and it also attracts dirt particles to garments. The best solution for reducing static is to wear fabrics made from blends or natural fibres.

Dribbling and other Moisture Problems

An inability to swallow saliva is a problem associated with a number of different disabilities. If saliva escapes, clothing can become anything from damp to very wet dependent upon the severity of the problem. There are numerous methods of minimizing the discomfort constant dampness can cause, but all depend in the first instance upon absorbent fabrics. Whatever the inherent absorbency of a fibre, this can be increased by the methods of yarn construction. A loose weave or knit will offer a greater surface area to absorb moisture, as

will a looped construction such as cotton towelling. Probably the most absorbent fabrics are wool melton and mouflon, fabrics used to produce quality duffle coats. The wool fibre is deliberately milled or felted during manufacture to create a very dense fabric. A milled tweed has similar properties. However, all these fabrics are relatively expensive, require dry cleaning, and can be very heavy.

The ability of a fabric to absorb saliva is not the sole consideration. Many people suffer chest infections caused by constant dampness, so ideally moisture should be prevented from penetrating to the chest. An absorbent outer fabric backed with a moisture-proof fabric can be the solution. The expanding sport and leisure market has led to a vast increase in the development and production of such waterproof fabrics.

If a waterproof fabric presents a complete barrier to moisture then any moisture produced by the body will come up against this barrier, condense and soak back into clothing and to the skin. This happens with conventional polyurethane or neoprane-coated fabrics. Some fabrics, mainly produced for sport and leisure-wear, are constructed to prevent rain droplets from penetrating from the outside, but will allow water vapour produced by the body to pass through, thus preventing a condensation problem. Such fabrics are generally referred to as 'breathable'. Fine woven cotton 'Ventile' is breathable, but does not cope with heavy rain or moisture. It can, however, be useful as a fabric backing if dribbling is light. Versatech is the trade name of a fine woven nylon which is breathable and waterproof. As with Ventile, its properties do not deteriorate with wear, unlike coated or laminated fabrics, which can crack and peel with washing and wear.

The expansion of the sport and leisure industry has led to increased research and development of specialist hi-tech fabrics, many of which have wider applications for other sections of the community, including the disabled. The following descriptions of four major types of 'hi-tech' fabric should give help to disabled people who experience moisture problems.

Microporous polyurethane coatings

Microporous honeycomb film is applied directly on to a nylon or polycotton face fabric, making it both waterproof and breathable. Carrington's 'Cyclone' is an example of this type of fabric. Careful laundering is necessary to prevent the ultra-fine holes from becoming clogged and then allowing water through.

Microporous membranes

A microporous laminated 'sandwich' of fabric which is waterproof and breathable. However, these laminates will not outlive a polyurethane-coated fabric of similar weight. 'Gore-tex' is the best known of these fabrics, but is only available to the garment industry.

Hydrophilic coatings

A polyurethane coating without pores, so that no cold moisture can pass through from the outside. However it is chemically modified so that humid water vapour surrounding the body is passed through the fabric to the outside and released into the air. This gives the fabric superior 'breathability' to conventional polyurethane coatings, but it is equally durable. Although not generally available, one hydrophilic-coated fabric is marketed under the 'Peter Storm' name and is well-known to walkers and ramblers.

Hydrophilic membranes

The membrane is thinner than a hydrophilic coating, so the breathability rating is higher. It is a solid film, therefore it avoids the possible clogging problem of microporous

coatings. It is not available on the retail market as yet, but can be obtained through Disability Clothing Workshops. It is marketed under the name of 'Sympatex' and is relatively expensive, but the washability, wear and high performance even after soaking in household bleach, can make the outlay worthwhile. It is particularly helpful for smaller items, such as trainer pants or garments which give protection from dribbling.

The majority of these specialist 'hi-tech' fabrics is not easily available to the individual, but the best way of obtaining fabric is through Fashion Services for the Disabled, who liaise with some of the specialist fabric manufacturers. Useful addresses are included on pp. 119–20. A useful source of garments made from these specialist fabrics are outdoor pursuits centres, some of whom provide a mail order service.

Wear and Tear

Calipers, braces and artificial limbs can cause severe wear on garments at the points where the jointing mechanisms, buckles or velcro catch or rub. Propelling wheelchairs or walking with crutches causes fabric fatigue at the cuffs or under the arms. Unusual ways of walking can cause wear between thighs, and crawling or bottom shuffling will also cause excessive wear. Strong fabrics such as denim or nylon, or any blended fabric containing more than 50 per cent nylon or polyester, wear well. If synthetic fabrics are undesirable because a degree of absorbency is essential then patches either inside or outside a garment in a strong fabric may be appropriate. A major difficulty can be that tough fabrics produce bulky seams which may damage sensitive skins or cause pressure sores. In this case, clever design of the garment with careful positioning of the seams can reduce the problem.

Corduroy, generally considered to be a

tough fabric, is only as strong as its backing weave. Simply by holding a piece of the fabric up to the light, it is possible to see how flimsy or sturdy the fabric is.

All yarns have a certain degree of elasticity, but not all are resilient, i.e. will return to their original state. Natural fibres, particularly wool, have superior resilience. The construction of the fabric will determine if it will stretch and to what degree. Knitted fabrics stretch more than woven ones, although a fabric with a loose weave will allow a small degree of give. Knitted fabrics, however, can fail to return to their original shape after repeated wearing and washing.

A degree of stretch can be added to tightly woven fabrics such as denim by introducing a small percentage of elastane. This can reduce wear and tear and strain on seams. More importantly, stretch fabrics can make dressing very much easier for someone with limited movement and for carers helping with dressing.

Fabrics as Fire Hazards

Textile fires are common and often have fatal consequences. In Britain one in five fires ignites in textiles and some 300 people are killed annually. A classic cause of such fires is the careless use of cigarettes, pipes or matches. People with disabilities may be exposed to a greater risk from fire than able-bodied people, either because they are unable to move away quickly from the source of the fire, or because a lack of balance may increase the risk of falling on to a fire. In addition, reduced feeling or awareness may mean a person does not detect burning until severe damage has been done.

It is essential to assess the extent to which a person may be exposed to the risk of fire when choosing clothing or fabrics. As far as clothing is concerned, loose and voluminous garments present the greatest risk and will burn more readily than close-fitting garments. There is no fabric which will not burn at all, but those which smoulder for a long time, or melt and shrink away from the source of the fire are preferable to those which flare easily, provided they do not produce noxious fumes. Brushed or pile fabrics, or loosely woven fabrics can encourage the spread of a fire. This is known as flammability. Thick yarns and close, thick weaves can reduce the flammability, of a fabric. Fabrics made from a mixture or blend of man-made and natural fibres – and these constitute a large proportion of fabrics available – will burn more quickly than any single one of the component fibres.

Untreated fabrics

Low risk:
Wool: smoulders and can self-extinguish
Modacrylic: modified acrylic, improved flame resistance
Polyester: slow to ignite; fuses and shrinks away from the flame
Chlorofibre: melts, but does not burn
N.B. Even in low-risk fabrics, starch, soap-based powders or fabric softeners can create build-up of coating on fibres which will increase flammability.

High risk:
Acrylic: flames rapidly, splutters and melts
Polyamide (nylon): burns slowly but with flaming molten droplets
Cotton: burns rapidly
Silk: burns, melts slowly and splutters
Rayon: burns quickly
Acetate and triacetate: burns quickly, splutters and melts, drips like burning tar

Treated fabrics

Almost any fabric can be treated to reduce flammability. There are two types of flame-retardant fabric, coated or inherent. Coated fabrics, for example Proban cotton, are inexpensive and comfortable to wear, but are not strong. The protection offered by the flame-retardant coating is not permanent and deteriorates as the garment is washed or dry cleaned. Inherent flame-retardant fabrics are those in which the fibres are treated before the fabric is woven or knitted. They give permanent protection, but are more expensive, generally not as easy to wear and need careful laundering.

Fabric Care

It is not always possible to identify a fabric just by looking at it. Natural and synthetic fibres can be used singly or in a huge variety of blends. They can imitate all kinds of fabric weave, and modern furnishing techniques can also modify the way a fabric should be handled and laundered. Occasionally fabrics have washing symbols printed along the selvedge, but if not it is as well to ask for washing instructions, or make sure of the fibre content, when buying the fabric. The international care labelling code gives clear instructions for washing and lists the fibre content on ready-made garments, but for piece-bought fabrics the following guidelines should help.

Fabric blends require different laundering from fabric mixtures. A fabric blend should be washed at the temperature appropriate to the fibre with the highest content in the blend. For example, a fabric with 60 per cent polyester, 35 per cent cotton and 5 per cent viscose should be washed at the correct temperature for polyester. Fabric mixtures should be washed in accordance with the fibre requiring the milder treatment. Therefore a polyester/wool mixture should be washed in warm suds because of the wool content.

Colour fastness

An easy test for colour fastness is to dampen a piece of spare fabric or the hem or seam allowance of the finished garment and then iron a piece of dry white fabric or paper towel over it. If any colour blots off wash the garment seperately in very cool suds and rinse at once in cold water, then spin and dry the garment as quickly as possible to avoid excessive colour loss. If the colour is very loose dry cleaning is preferable, provided the fabric is not one which is specifically precluded from this method.

Soaking

It is sometimes necessary to soak a garment to remove stubborn stains or heavy soiling. This should be done in cool water to avoid colour loss. White and coloured garments should not be soaked together. White nylon in particular should be soaked and washed separately as it takes up both colour and dirt very easily from other articles. There should be sufficient water for articles to be moved around freely. Wool, silk or fabrics with a flame-resistant finish should never be soaked.

The international care labelling code

The basic symbols:

For washing (by hand or machine)

For tumble-drying (after washing)

For dry cleaning

For bleaching

For ironing. The number of dots on the ironing symbol indicates the correct temperature setting – the fewer the dots the cooler the setting.

If any of these symbols has a cross over it, it means 'do not' use this process.

Dry cleaning symbols:

(A) Fabric normal for dry cleaning in all solvents

(P) Fabric normal for dry cleaning in perchloroethylene, Solvent R113, white spirit and Solvent R11

(F) Fabric normal for dry cleaning in Solvent R113 and white spirit.

N.B.

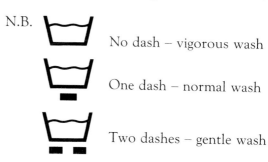

No dash – vigorous wash

One dash – normal wash

Two dashes – gentle wash

In 1986 the care labelling code numbers used on garment and textile labels were amended to a series of bar symbols which are used throughout the European Community.

OLD	NEW	Examples of Application
1/95	95	White cotton and linen articles without special finishes
2/60	60	Cotton, linen or viscose articles without special finishes where colours are fast at 60°C
3/60	60	(Not used in UK) White nylon and white polyester/cotton mixtures are included in 50
4/50	50	Nylon; polyester/cotton mixture; polyester cotton and viscose articles with special finishes; cotton/acrylic mixtures
5/40	40	Cotton, linen or viscose articles, where colours are fast at 40°C but not at 60°C
6/40	40	Acrylics, acetate and triacetate, including mixtures with wool; polyester/wool blends
7/40	40	Wool, wool mixed with other fibres; silk
8/30	30	(Not used in UK) See items included in 40 and 40
9/95	95	(Not applicable in UK)
(handwash)	(handwash)	Handwash (Do not machine wash)
(do not wash)	(do not wash)	Do not wash

4 UNDERSTANDING THE PROBLEMS

For those not working with people with a disability but who would be more than happy to use their expertise, it may be useful to look at some of the diseases associated with disability and at the various problems they create. Clothing problems arise from a medical situation, and a knowledge of this helps us to understand many of the problems which otherwise would not be seen. Knowledge also gives us some idea of the kind of questions we need to ask if we are to make, or help others to make, garments which meet all the needs of the individual, and it enables us to see the person as a person rather than as just a clothing problem. You cannot help in a sensitive way until you understand, and understanding takes away the fear that many people have of disability simply because they don't know what to expect, or what is expected of them.

Amputees

Lower limb amputations are the result of accident or illness. Fifty per cent of diabetics who smoke are amputees. People with one leg amputated usually have an artificial limb, but those with both legs amputated rarely do, because walking with two artificial limbs requires a great deal of energy.

Loss of an arm can be the result of an accident, a malignant tumour or a congenital deformity like thalidomide. We use our hands to supplement our speech and express our feelings as well as to carry on our daily tasks, so they become very much a part of our personality. Hands are always within our sight, thus the disfigurement is always visible, and this can have varying psychological effects on the individual.

Arthritis

Arthritis is a chronic inflammatory disease of the joints which limits movement and causes considerable pain. The joints are often enlarged. Osteoarthritis begins in the larger joints, the hips and shoulders, whereas rheumatoid arthritis begins in the smaller joints. The latter is most common in middle-aged people and affects four times as many women as men. Sufferers may have difficulty holding things, standing can be painful, walking is painful and difficult. Some people eventually become wheelchair-bound. There can be weakness and deformity in shoulders, fingers, knees, ankles, toes and hips. Those with arthritis often have difficulty in getting dressed and undressed because of having to move their shoulders and raise their arms. Fastenings, especially small ones, can also be difficult, as is putting on shoes and stockings. Keeping warm is a major problem. Shape problems can also arise, for instance when shoulders become elevated and so shorten the neck, knee joints are enlarged, or when some people become bent over from hip level.

Cerebral Palsy

This is a form of paralysis resulting from damage to the part of the brain which controls the muscles. It can happen before, during, or after birth. There are three kinds of cerebral palsy: spastic, athetoid, and ataxic. Spasticity is a stiffness in the muscles making limbs rigid and very difficult to dress. Athetoid creates uncontrollable movements and posture, and the ataxic have difficulty in co-ordinating movements. People with cerebral palsy can be highly intelligent but they can have difficulty in communicating and this can disguise their mental ability. However, mental subnormality is not uncommon. All people with cerebral palsy need extra time to do things, but other help will depend on the type and extent of the disability. They may need help with transportation, feeding, toileting and dressing. It is vital to keep warm and, as many over-salivate, they need protection for their clothing. Shape problems can arise from the rigid limbs of the spastic and the floppy posture of the athetoid.

Downs Syndrome

This is also known as mongolism and is a congenital abnormality. A Downs Syndrome has 47 chromosomes instead of the normal 46, and this causes defects of physical and mental development. Body proportion is different; they have broad faces, short, thick necks, short stature, put on weight easily and have loose limbs. Fingers tend to be clumsy and create fastening problems. A Downs Syndrome child can be trained to overcome incontinence, but where co-ordination is difficult, clothes need to be easy to put on and take off to allow Downs Syndromes to be independent.

Dwarfing Diseases

Abnormally reduced size is caused by a disorder of the pituitary gland and a lack of growth hormone. The figure can be small but in proportion, which means they have great difficulty in finding clothing to suit their age, or they can have short arms and legs in relation to body size. This latter group need standard body sizes but sleeve and leg lengths are far too big. Many people from both groups find they need to have their garments made to measure.

Mental Handicap

Mental handicap is a result of brain damage which can arise from a number of causes. The degree of handicap varies tremendously but many people, with training, are able to look after themselves. Their clothes need to be easy to put on, with fastenings placed where they can be seen, and they take a longer time to dress.

Mental Illness

In this area there are psychiatric problems which create clothing difficulties of a totally different nature to other disabilities. Some people pick at their clothing and manage to remove the stitching from seams and collars, while others chew their clothing. There are those people who bite themselves and need protective clothing. Some may take off their clothes, given the opportunity, and they need garments with fastenings which are out of sight and out of reach. Where visual problems are also involved some people are a fire risk, for example putting a half-smoked cigarette into their pocket without extinguishing it properly. For these people, fire-resistant fabrics need to be sought.

Multiple Sclerosis

Patches of damage to the nervous tissue develop throughout the nervous system. These patches flare up and then take weeks or months to settle down. Symptoms are a sudden weakness in one or both lower limbs, visual problems, and numbness in the affected areas. The symptoms can return within weeks or years, the person becoming more disabled with each attack. The cause is unknown. It usually starts in adult life and affects more women than men. In the later stages sufferers can have poor or no vision, are incontinent, confined to a wheelchair, and are unable to feed or dress themselves. Clothes should be easy to put on and involve the disabled person in as little lifting as possible, and fastenings need to be of a type that helps the person to be independent for as long as possible.

Muscular Dystrophy

This is a progressive wasting disease of the muscles. It is hereditary, resulting from a genetic defect in metabolism. It affects only boys, and appears between birth and six years of age. As it spreads, people become more and more helpless and need to be dressed, toileted, and generally looked after. They do not suffer pain. Eventually they will become wheelchair-bound. They will need clothing which is easy to put on and fastenings which are easy for them or the carer. Some people get very heavy and so the positioning of fastenings becomes important. They should give easy access without being placed in areas where the person will lean against them, as this could create pressure sores.

Poliomyelitis

Poliomyelitis is an acute infection of the central nervous system caused by a virus. It attacks the nerves controlling the muscles and sometimes results in paralysis or partial paralysis to one or more limbs. Sufferers may need to use a wheelchair or walk with the aid of sticks or crutches. It is a static disability which does not get worse.

Scoliosis and Kyphosis

Scoliosis is a sideways curvature of the spine, while kyphosis is a hump back. These disabilities can be the result of some other disease but in many cases there is no known cause. Many elderly people with a scoliosis have become deformed because the correcting operation, which involves putting a rod into the spine, has only been available in recent years. With less severe cases, early treatment like wearing a brace, or electrical stimulation of the muscles, can prevent the curvature from getting worse. Some people may have to wear padding, and often they feel very self-conscious about their shape. They cannot move quickly and they tend to feel the cold. The main clothing problem is to get garments to hang correctly. In some cases it is necessary to fit the garment to a brace rather than to a person, and clever ideas are needed to detract the eye away from the appliance. Appliances also create wear and tear problems.

Spina Bifida

A congenital malformation of the spine, occurring in the early embryonic period and often causing deformity and paralysis. Legs can be short and deformed. Severity depends on the level of damage, varying from a small patch of numbness to complete paralysis from the waist down. Spina bifida is often associated with hydrocephalus (water on the brain), and the head can be slightly larger than normal. Nowadays, a shunt is fitted into the neck to correct the flow of water. Drugs may be used to control fits. Many young people may be in wheelchairs, or walk with difficulty using sticks or other forms of support. Their upper limbs appear to be strong and unaffected and may become well-developed through pushing wheelchairs.

There are hidden defects which affect learning, such as spacial, visual or perceptual awareness, sequencing difficulties and a poor concept of time and memory. All affect manipulative tasks and make it difficult to complete routines successfully and to reason logically. Fastenings may be a problem for some people. Many have incontinence problems and may wear pads, have a catheter fitted, or have stomas, following operations for bladder and/or bowel diversions. These involve bags attached to the abdomen which need to be emptied and changed. Spina bifida sufferers' circulation is very poor and they need to be kept warm. Because many people are unable to feel changes in temperature they need to be protected from burning themselves. Safety is a primary requirement for clothing, mostly related to sticks and wheelchairs or to lack of feeling. Calipers also create a wear problem. There are difficulties related to shape and proportion, and allowance must be made, and easy access provided, for incontinence pads and appliances.

Spinal Injuries

The main cause of spinal injuries is road traffic accidents and, consequently, many young, fit people are affected. The damage is to the spinal cord, and the higher up the spine the damage occurs the more disabled the person will be. People with spinal injuries are often wheelchair-bound and often incontinent. When the paralysis is in the legs only they are known as paraplegics, but when all four limbs are affected they are tetraplegics or quadraplegics. Many are unable to dress themselves or help in any way. They suffer from excessive sweating and they are unable to control their body temperature, so non-absorbent, synthetic fibres must be avoided. When designing garments,

seams must be carefully positioned to avoid pressure sores, and help given to the carer to aid dressing.

Strokes

A stroke is a one-sided paralysis, partial or complete, resulting from the interruption of the blood supply to the brain. The cause may be obstruction by a clot in a blood vessel supplying the brain, or the rupture of a vessel with consequent bleeding into the brain tissue. Speech may be affected. There may be problems of mental and/or emotional confusion and changes of personality are very common. Balance can also be a problem and walking can be difficult or impossible. Personal care and all activities of daily life become much more difficult with only one hand. Dressing is a slow and frustrating process, and certain garments, bras, for example are impossible to put on without adaptation. Fastenings need to be of a type and in a position suited to the wearer. Fabrics should be easy to care for to assist independence. A good way to appreciate these problems, and eventually to solve them, is to put yourself in the place of the person you are working with, and find out what you can or cannot do with only one hand.

Visual Impairment

People with little or no sight may also have other disabilities to consider. Even if they do not, they will need to be able to distinguish the back of the garment from the front by label, motif, etc. They can choose fabrics by their texture, but they also need to be involved in the choice of style and colour. They may not 'see' but they do visualize what garments look like and a friend or relative who is prepared to explain styles and colours when out shopping is invaluable.

The range of problems we need to consider when designing and making clothing with the disabled is quite considerable. It covers shape, size and proportion, amputation, restricted movement, loss of manipulative skills, excessive cold and heat, wear and tear of garments by appliances or by means of transportation, incontinence, safety, and accessibility to appliances. From this it is easy to realize that garments need to be well made, in good-quality fabrics, because they get far more wear and tear and washing than do garments made for the able-bodied.

The list of problems may sound formidable, but many of them can be solved quite simply once you have established what the problems and the needs of the individual are. Pointers for discussion will be what kind of fastenings can be managed and where they should be positioned, what styles and fabrics are sympathetic to the wearer's personality and needs, and what necessary alterations can be done without spoiling the look and balance of the garment.

Finding an answer to one problem may exacerbate another. With their help, we need to list the clothing problems experienced by disabled people, and find out from them which problems they can live with and which ones cause them the most difficulty. Then, together, with the help of clever design and mixture fabrics, you will be able to solve the problems satisfactorily.

5 FINDING THE SOLUTIONS

Having looked at various disabilities and the many clothing problems they present, we must now find solutions to these problems. Some solutions may come to us easily, others can take a long time, but for every problem and every person there is an answer. Two people may appear to have the same problem, but it does not follow that the same solution will work for both of them. Differing shapes, manipulative skills and degrees of mobility, must all be taken into consideration.

Not all solutions involve alterations to patterns or clothing. After trial and error, the majority of us find a manufacturer whose garments seem to fit us better than most, or a pattern company whose patterns are nearest to our shape. It is surprising how sizes differ from one manufacturer to another but, as a rule of thumb, more expensive garments have more room, with larger seam and hem allowances, while cheaper garments are smaller with less ease, and give little scope for minor alterations. Often we realize that certain types of sleeve, bodice, neckline, skirt, jacket or trousers suit our shape best, and so the correct choice of style can be all that is needed. On the other hand, other disabled people have commented that not only are they unable to buy clothing to fit, they cannot buy patterns either, so although they may be able to sew they need help and advice to use their skills to good effect.

This chapter offers solutions that have worked for a number of people with varying clothing problems whom we have met and worked with at Fashion Services for the Disabled. Some of the suggestions may seem so simple that you wonder why you haven't thought of them before. But even if there should be nothing that meets your particular need you will undoubtedly have some positive ideas by the end of the chapter, and could be well on the way to finding your own answers.

All alterations to garments and patterns referred to and illustrated in this chapter are explained in more detail in the chapters on pattern and clothing alterations later on in the book. Suitable types of fabric for each problem area will be found in the previous chapter on fabrics.

Wear and Tear

Wear and tear is mainly caused by appliances, wheelchairs, crawling and shuffling, dribbling, incontinence, excessive general use and laundering. I remember once asking a group of mothers of spina bifida children what clothing problems they had. They informed me they didn't have any, yet one mother said, 'My little boy wears a pair of trousers through in a day, would you call that a problem?' The child wore calipers and crawled, so there was friction from the outside as he moved around the floor and friction from the inside as his calipers rubbed against the fabric. For other people the wear is either from the inside or from the outside, but even then clothes wear through very quickly and create extra repair work and expense.

22 Patches for a child

When working with children the scope for strengthening garments is endless. Patches in the right places and in the right fabrics give the garment a longer life, and they can also be very attractive. They needn't be just round or square, but can take the shape of balloons or the child's favourite toy or animal (Fig. 22). The motif can be repeated on pockets, bib fronts, etc., and become part of the design of the garment rather than purely a functional patch. A padded motif gives added comfort and protection. When the patch shows signs of wear it can easily be exchanged for another one. The elephant can acquire a howdah, the kangaroo a baby in the pocket. Quite simply, you can let your imagination run riot.

For an older person, we may need to be a little more restrained. A patch of a contrasting colour or texture in a hard-wearing fabric can be attractive or, if you wish to be more functional, stretch patches with a suede look are available from haberdashery stores, as are ski patches in an elasticated nylon fabric, which give hard wear, stretch and an attract-

ive appearance. Both stretch and ski patches are washable. Patches in iron-on denim, corduroy or a plain grey suiting fabric are also available. The addition of a row of stitching around the outside gives them longer life. When clothes wear out quickly there is a temptation to buy cheaper ones. These will wear through even faster. Closely woven fabrics, which are better quality and therefore will be more expensive, will last longer and are worth adapting.

Appliances

If the wear is from the inside, for example with calipers or artificial limbs, patches need to be on the inside. Double fabric can be used in the area of excessive wear if you are making your own garments, or patches can be stitched or ironed on. The suede-look patches are good where calipers rub. Alternatively, you can line or part line the garment with nylon or polyester to take the wear away from the garment itself. It is much cheaper to replace a lining than to buy a new skirt, dress or pair of trousers. But make sure the fabric you use is suited to the other requirements. A slippery lining can assist in transferring from chair to car, but if the wearer cannot control his or her movements such a lining could be counter-productive. Likewise, excessive sweating will not be absorbed by nylon or polyester fabrics and can cause discomfort and sores. In cases like these, mixture fabrics like polycotton would be the best choice for a lining fabric.

Wheelchairs

Sleeves can get very dirty and worn from pushing wheelchairs, especially on wet days. There are jackets on the market with zip-in sleeves so that the garment doubles up as a body warmer. This enables the sleeves to be washed more often than the garment. It may be worth contacting the manufacturers to see if they would be prepared to supply extra sleeves. Some jackets have sleeves in sections attached by poppers, which again allow easy laundering of excessively dirty areas. If you are making your own anoraks or leisure jackets you could make two or three sets of sleeves.

If the sleeves in a ready-made jacket are too long it is possible to remove excess length just above the elbow. You can adjust the width of the top half of the sleeve until it matches the shortened lower half, and then fasten the lower sleever back on with poppers or a zip to give the correct length. At the same time you could take a pattern from the bottom section and make other sleeves in contrasting colours (Fig. 23).

Wheelchair straps that fasten with Velcro often leave an area of the velcro hooks uncovered, which can catch on clothing and pull threads. One solution is to stick a piece of leather over the top, but an alternative, useful idea for covering the excess Velcro is to make a purse with a loop that the strap slots through (Fig. 24).

Seams on socks can create wear and tear on delicate skins. Legs and feet may be chubby or long and thin, and it is often difficult to find a pair of socks that fits correctly. Knitted spiral socks have no seams and can be made to any width or length in any yarn. Instructions for these are given on p. 105.

Dribbling

Dribbling is a problem for many disabled people. Very often it can create a sore chin or a chest cold, and it is not pleasant to have a continually soggy and discoloured front. Clothing must be changed often – a time-consuming task – and constant washing of

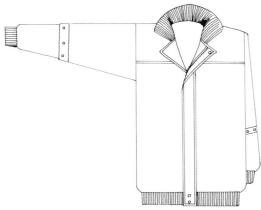

23 Method of shortening a sleeve for wheelchair users

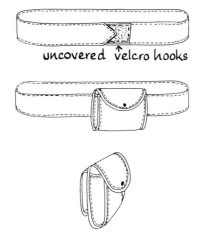

24 Covering Velcro in a useful way

25 Ideas for those who salivate a little

garments will wear them out quickly. All too often, bibs are worn to absorb moisture, protect the clothing and cut down on washing and changing, but they do remind us of babyhood, and if we are not very careful our attitude towards people wearing bibs can cause distress.

If the problem is slight, bows and scarves for women (Figs. 25a and 25b), and a cravat for men (Fig. 25c), could be the answer. These can absorb the moisture and can be changed quickly. It is useful to remember that patterned fabrics do not become so obviously wet as plain fabrics.

If the problem is more severe make a note of the area of clothing that gets wet and consider what can be done to solve the problem. It mustn't have the appearance of a bib, yet it must serve the same purpose. Perhaps a collar, or a protective front may be the answer. Whatever is chosen must be absorbent at the front, waterproof at the back, and look as though it is part of the

garment it is covering. Collars can have tucks, lace or embroidery and be very flattering; sporty clothes like tracksuits and sweatshirts can have poppered- or buttoned-on sections, or a complete front which fastens to the original garment at waist level with D-rings and Velcro. Men can have false shirt fronts similar to the ones worn in the 1930s. A tabard can be a useful garment to make for wearing over blouses, shirts or jumpers, and looks smart with skirts or trousers (Fig. 26).

Incontinence

This can be a distressing, embarrassing problem, which can lead to social problems, but it doesn't have to. There are now many Continence Advisers throughout the country who know what help is available, and who will work with you to solve your problem. So don't suffer in silence!

Many disabled people who are not incon-

26 Protective fronts for those who salivate

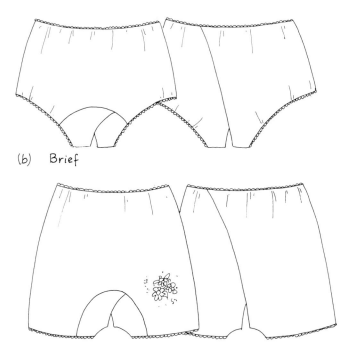

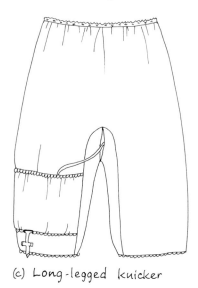

(b) Brief

(a) Pantie

(c) Long-legged knicker

27 Open-crotch knickers

tinent have accidents from time to time. This is often because it takes a long time to get to the toilet, manipulating clothing is difficult, or lack of co-ordination or concentration can make fastenings awkward to use in a hurry. All too often, women stop wearing knickers to make toileting easier. Embarrassment can cause them to become housebound, affecting their social life and that of their partner. There has to be a better answer!

Pleated or softly gathered skirts, or self-lined skirts with a A-line or slight flare are easier to manage than tight skirts or skirts that are too full, and they will not need a petticoat. Stockings can be better than tights, although single-leg and open-crotch tights are available. French knickers can be pushed to one side, while open-crotch knickers do not need to be removed. You can make your own open-crotch knickers from the patterns shown on pp. 102–5. Made in pretty fabrics with a bit of lace, they can be attractive as well as functional, and they do a lot for the morale (Fig. 27). They will also solve the problem.

Women who wear hip-length calipers have difficulty getting knicker or pant legs over the top of the calipers to pull them down. They wear out very quickly and often tear if there is urgency. French knickers may be the answer, or you can adapt ordinary knickers by making an opening in the crotch seam (Fig. 28).

Men who are wheelchair-bound and use a urinal bottle also have accidents. These can be eliminated if a longer zip is put into the trousers to extend the opening to the crotch seam. Y-fronts can be difficult to manipulate, but trunks are much easier as the front overwrap goes right down to the crotch seam. There is a row of stitching across the overwrap 5 cm (2 in.) higher than the crotch seam, but this can be removed to extend the opening and the overwrap restitched nearer to the crotch (Fig. 29).

Boys and men who have difficulty unfastening trousers quickly need to look for half elastic or fully elasticated waistbands which will enable them to pull the trousers down quickly. It is essential that they are men's trousers with a fly front and not ladies trousers, otherwise this will do nothing for

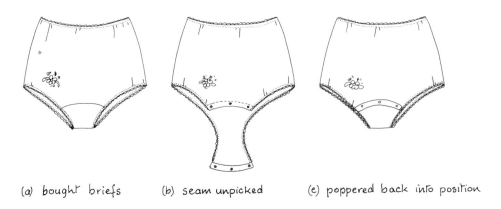

(a) bought briefs   (b) seam unpicked   (c) poppered back into position

28 Altering knickers for hip-length calipers

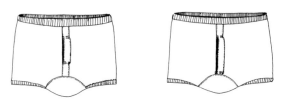

29 Extending fly opening in trunks

their morale. It is possible to replace the zip with Velcro spots but as the trousers tend to be washed very frequently the spots soon lose their grip.

Men who have had a stroke, or who have only one arm will find manipulating trousers a very frustrating business. A piece of elastic threaded through the waistband to form a circle enables trousers to remain part way down the legs when toileting instead of falling to the floor, and also facilitates the fastening of the waistband and zip (Fig. 30b).

People using a catheter bag need easy access for emptying the bag. Men's trousers can have a short zip set into the inside leg seam at the appropriate place (Fig. 30a). A pocket can be placed on the inside of the trouser leg, near to the ankle, to hold the bag in position. A hole in the base of the pocket will accommodate the tube used to empty the bag. A person using this method needs to have good balance, and the bag needs to be emptied frequently as it can get heavy and spoil the hang of the trousers. Older women

may like to wear open-crotch, long-legged knickers with a pocket placed on one leg (Fig. 27c).

A good trouser style for people with a stoma is one with pleats in the front, which give extra fabric allowance over the stoma bag. To empty stoma bags easily, trousers can have zips fitted into each side seam, approximately 30 cm (12 in.) long. Elastic is inserted through the back waistband and fastens at the front with a button. When the zips are unfastened the front of the trousers drops forward, giving easy access to the bag (Fig. 31b). Fig. 31a shows trousers designed to accommodate a broomstick plaster.

This trouser adaption can also be helpful to people who need help with toileting. The method can be reversed to drop the back of the trousers, but care must be taken to ensure that the back flap is well out of the way. Women may like to consider wearing a kilt-style skirt back to front. The pleats are attractive to look at, the overwrap is flat to sit on and can be drawn to one side, with the ends tucked into the waistband before toileting. Alternatively, the kilt can be worn normally, as with any wrap-over style, and then undone and left on a chair while transferring to the toilet. It is one less garment to manoeuvre and is in position on the chair ready to sit on and fasten again quickly. Each person will find a method which works best for her.

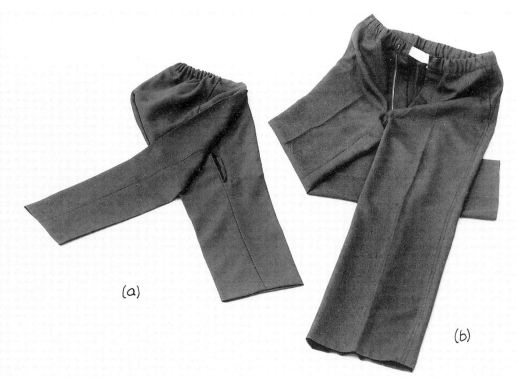

30 *above* Zip in trouser seam/elastic waist
for use with one hand

31 *below* Trousers for broomstick plaster
and trousers for stomas

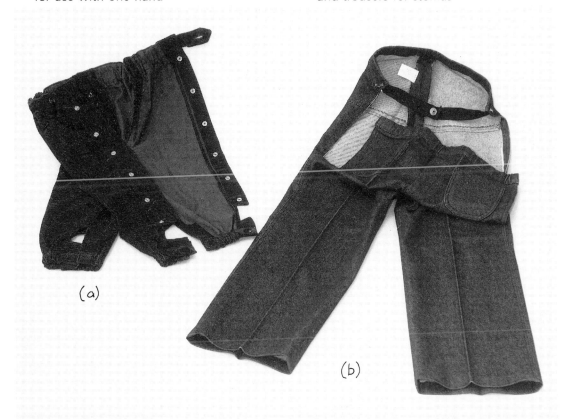

With personal freshness in mind, many people wear polyester trousers because they wash easily and dry quickly. Unfortunately, no matter how well they are washed, they do retain odour. A mixture of polyester and worsted or acrylic should wash well and reduce the problem of odour.

Manipulative Problems

Anyone who has restricted movement in the shoulder joints or has lost the ability to grip or feel, or whose finger joints are stiff, will have problems getting in and out of garments and fastening them independently. Similar problems arise if you have had a stroke and need to dress with only one hand, or if you have lost a hand or were born without hands.

Foundation garments

Foundation garments, in particular, can be a nightmare. Reaching round to the back to fasten a bra is impossible for many people. There are some sports bras on the market that have no fastenings, and a stretch lace pull-on bra, but these are not for the well-endowed. Some people put the bra round them back to front, fasten the hooks, and then slide it back into position, but a front-fastening bra can make life much easier. Even then, hooks and eyes are small and difficult to manage, especially with only one hand. You may find it helpful to take the hooks away from a front-fastening bra and insert a zip which is 13–16 cm (5–6 in.) longer than the opening. This enables the bra to open out and gives you much more room to put it on. A ribbon loop on the bottom of the zip can be slotted over the finger or thumb of a paralyzed hand to anchor the zip, while a loop attached to the tab will help you pull up the zip. A back-fastening bra can be treated

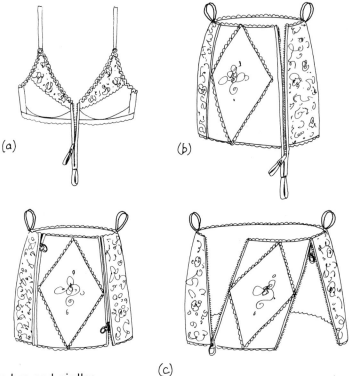

(a)

(b)

(c)

32 Alteration to bra and girdles

in the same way by removing the hooks, closing the back and inserting a zip in the front. A bra-slip is another useful garment which can be altered to accommodate a front-fastening zip. In each case an overlock, stretch or zig-zag stitch will strengthen the new seams (Fig. 32a).

A side-fastening girdle can be treated in a similar way to a bra. Remove the hooks and insert a longer zip to allow the garment to open wider for easier dressing. If you find bending difficult, two loops stitched on to the sides of the girdle at the top will allow you to get the garment down to your feet, and will assist in pulling on the garment (Fig. 32b). Another method with a step-in girdle is the insertion of two zips, one from the top down to within 2.5 cm (1 in.) of the bottom of the garment, and one from the bottom up

to within 2.5 cm (1 in.) of the top of the girdle. This also allows the garment to open wider. Loops on the zip tabs always make fastening easier (Fig. 32c).

You may find a girdle uncomfortable if you sit all day, but it is possible to shape the garment to eliminate this discomfort. Wear the girdle for a while and then check whether the top rolls over, the bottom is uncomfortably tight at the front, or the suspenders need moving from the back to the sides. Some instructions for girdle alterations are given on pp. 106–7. Usually girdles are bought by waist size, but occasionally they are measured by the hip size.

33 Shirt with Velcro spots

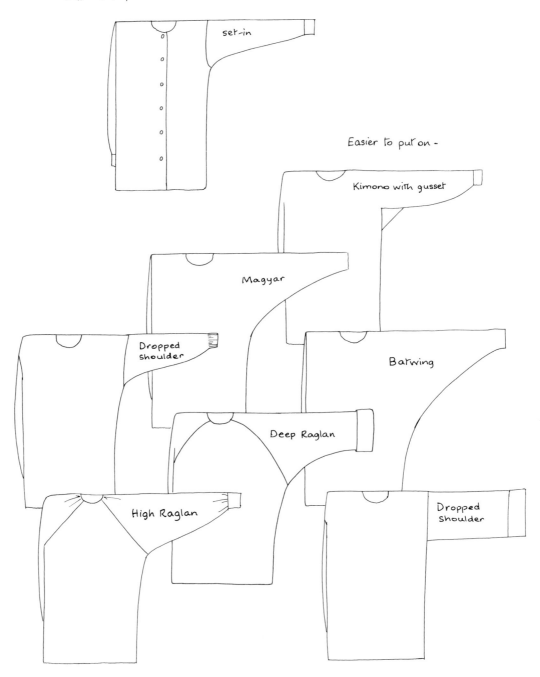

Difficult to put on –

set-in

Easier to put on –

Kimono with gusset

Magyar

Dropped shoulder

Batwing

Deep Raglan

High Raglan

Dropped Shoulder

34 Choice of sleeves

Shirts and blouses

These may have very small buttons which are extremely difficult to fasten. Larger buttons would make the garment look odd and unbalanced, so our aim must be to maintain, not alter, the appearance of the garment. Buttons can be removed and sewn on top of the buttonhole on the opposite side. Velcro spot-ons are then sewn underneath the buttonhole in place of the button (Fig. 33). Cuff buttons can be sewn on with a short shank of shirring elastic. Even when closed, this allows the cuff to stretch sufficiently for the hand to be put through. Alternatively, two buttons can be joined with shirring elastic on a longer shank to act as cufflinks. In each case, the buttons can be left fastened.

Blouses which fasten down the back are only useful if you need help with dressing. They can be invaluable for people with little or no movement in their arms or for those unable to lift their arms upwards or backwards, as they enable a person to be dressed from the back. This style is usually buttoned, and unless the buttons are very flat and well-positioned they could cause considerable discomfort if they were leant on for long periods. An open-ended zip would prove too bulky, so it is best to replace the buttons with Velcro spot-ons.

Dresses

The style of fastening on a dress will indicate how easy it is to put on. Front-fastening dresses with zips or large buttons are usually reasonably manageable. It is simple to check which shape of button is best for you, and changing the buttons may solve your problem and still suit the garment. Velcro spot-ons can be used, but they will pull apart if there is tension across the garment at any point.

Sleeves can be a problem if you need help with dressing. Some styles of sleeve are much easier to get into than others. A set-in sleeve is the tightest and most difficult (Fig. 34).

If fastenings are a major problem you may be able to choose a dress or a top with no fastenings. Many necklines enable you to get your head through easily, and if the fabric is knitted, or the style loose, this could solve any difficulties you may have (Fig. 35).

For those with severe dressing problems, a dress with a simple bodice style with no collar and a back zip will need the addition of a front fastening as well. This will enable the garment to be put over the head and dropped to the waist. There is then ample space to dress each arm and lift the dress into position for fastening (see Fig. 79 on p. 109).

Jackets and coats

With jackets and coats the major problems are getting into sleeves, manipulating fastenings, and the lifting and pushing involved in putting on a coat if you are wheelchair-bound. Many casual jackets have open-ended zips, which are not easy to fasten independently. If fastenings are the only difficulty jackets, being heavier-weight garments, can take larger, more manageable buttons. Some people may find toggles even easier to fasten.

Should you need help with dressing, consider opening the back seam of the garment from the hem to the collar and put in a fine zip or add an extension and Velcro spot-ons. This enables you to get your arms in more easily. If you are making a jacket the back fastening can go right through the collar as well, allowing the jacket to be put on in front. The front can remain partially fastened, be opened to give extra room for movement, or even separated into two halves if necessary (Figs. 36a and 36b).

A full-length coat is necessary in cold weather, but it does present problems for wheelchair users. You either lift yourself up with you arms while someone pushes the garment underneath you, or you need two people to lift you. It is not possible to tell

35 Choice of necklines

36a Open-back jacket   36b

whether the garment is straight underneath, or whether you have been left sitting on bunched-up fabric. One answer to this it to cut off the back of the coat at chair level and leave the front of the coat normal length (Fig. 37).

Vents in the side seams are advisable if the coat is a straight style. A fitting will soon show whether or not this is necessary. The appearance of the coat at the front can be checked to ensure there are not too many folds of fabric at hip level and there is no pull on the side seam. Adding side vents does not alter the appearance of the coat when being worn, in fact it sits better, is more comfortable to wear and can be put on without lifting. If you have little or no arm movement this idea, plus opening the back seam of the coat, makes dressing quicker and easier for both you and the carer and is invaluable if incontinence is also a problem.

37 Shortened coat back

Tracksuits

The insertion of knitted panels can also give extra room to help dressing. A tracksuit top can have panels added made from ribbed cuffing fabric which has much more stretch than the tracksuit itself. They can be in the same colour, or in a contrast. Decide where you are short of room when dressing. Do you need more stretch across your back, or in the sleeve, or under the arm? It is easy to design the garment accordingly. Similarly, hand-knitted panels in textured yarns can be let into woven garments and can look very attractive (Fig. 38).

For caliper wearers, short zips let into the side seams of tight-fitting trousers or tracksuits at the ankle allow the garment to be pulled over the top of boots. Similar openings in sleeve seams at the wrist give space for carers to draw arms through sleeves.

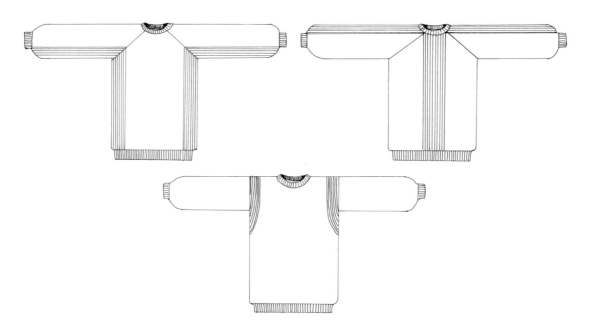

38a Letting in knitted panels

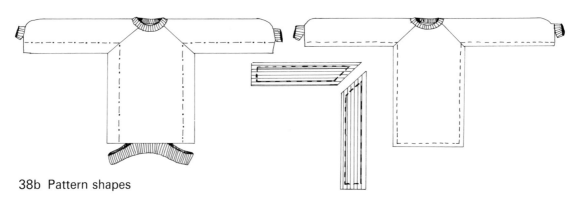

38b Pattern shapes

Warmth

Warmth is a major problem for many people. Garments need to be warm, but lightweight and not restrictive. The same applies to winter sportswear, and often the right garment can be found in shops selling sports and leisure-wear. If you see an advertisement for underwear, socks or anoraks that says 'Tested on Everest' it should provide you with the warmth you are seeking!

To keep legs warm you could make smart spats in fur or quilted fabric. These will fit over calipers and often look like boots. Alternatively, they can be made in thinner fabric to wear next to the skin underneath the calipers, and the trousers can be worn over the top (Fig. 39a). Spiral knitted socks are well-fitted, warm, and can be any length (Fig. 39b).

Hands are often cold, but sometimes gloves can be too bulky for manipulative work, or even for driving a car. There are fingerless gloves on the market which allow the thumbs to be free as well. They have a pouch which fastens on to the back of the hand and provides extra warmth, but can be brought over the fingers to form a mitten when needed. These are made for people who go shooting, and sports shops should be able to obtain them for you. There is also a Sirdar knitting pattern available to enable you to knit your own gloves. You need to finish the thumb and add ribbing to bring it just above the joint, rather than complete the thumb as in the pattern (Fig. 39c).

For all problems of warmth, the choice of fabric is vitally important (see pp. 30–3).

39 Spats, socks and gloves

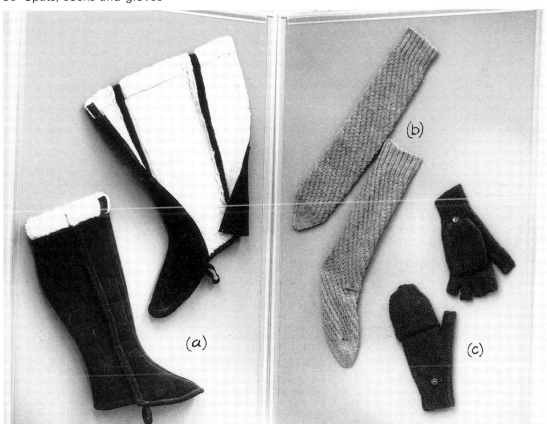

Shape, Size, Proportion

Body shapes change because of the way we live and the work we do. Carrying heavy shoulder bags always on the same shoulder lowers that shoulder, carrying babies around on one hip can make the hips asymmetrical, jobs that require a lot of lifting develop arm and chest muscles, and those which necessitate a lot of bending over have an effect on our backs. These problems are more pronounced for people who are disabled, and they have great difficulty finding garments that fit correctly and hang properly. The following suggestions are related to specific areas of disability but, as indicated above, their application can be of much wider use.

Single leg amputations

If you wear an artificial limb, trousers and skirts need to be larger around the waist to accommodate the waistband of the limb. Fully- or half-elasticated waists on skirts or trousers made from hard-wearing fabric are thought to be the best. It is also easy to alter trouser and skirt patterns at the waistline (see pp. 85–6).

Double leg amputations

Quite understandably, people like to put on a whole pair of trousers. It is an important boost to their morale. So what to do with the trouser legs becomes as much a psychological as a practical problem. Each person must decide what is acceptable to him. Normally, he would only see himself as far as the edge of the wheelchair but it is better, from an aesthetic point of view, to place himself in front of a mirror and discuss with family or carer how he should accommodate excess trouser legs.

Some men find shortened trouser legs acceptable but others prefer to wear a regular trouser and either fold the extra fabric back and sit on it, or fold it forward and tuck the trouser legs into their waistband, or roll them up and fasten them with safety pins. This last method can be practical but, unless the safety pins are hidden, is unsightly and somewhat 'Heath Robinson'. Trouser legs must on no account be left hanging as they become a safety hazard. The perfect answer might be to wear a kilt!

Women do not have the same problem. They often prefer to wear longer, fuller skirts. Their problem can be one of balance, for example when transferring from the wheelchair to another seat, especially if a lot of fabric has to be got out of the way. Therefore skirt styles need to be slightly flared, pleated, or softly gathered to drape nicely and give room for movement without having too much fullness. Younger people of both sexes may find they like the look of smart, pleated and cuffed Bermuda shorts for casual as well as sports-wear.

Single arm amputations

People with an artificial arm often prefer to wear long sleeves. A sleeve tucked into a pocket is less obvious if no artificial arm is worn, but the choice should be left to the individual. A lot depends on where the amputation is, and whether the remaining arm is of use to the person. If this is the case it is important that clothing does not impede its use. However, sleeves which give more room facilitate dressing, and as an artificial arm wears fabric out quickly the extra fullness, not being in close contact with the limbs, will give the sleeve longer life.

People with the Thalidomide disability are extremely clever at using their feet and mouths to help themselves with dressing and other tasks. Should they need extra warmth, body warmers and sleeveless waistcoats are invaluable.

Kyphosis

A hump back requires extra fabric across the back and extra lengths between the neck and

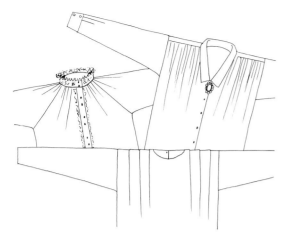

40a Neckline for kyphosis

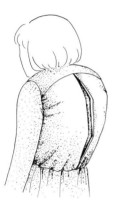

40b A style to avoid

41 Garment being worn (kyphosis)

waist. Garments bought to the correct bust or chest measurement feel tight and restricting and put a strain on armhole seams, and the waistline and hemlines are lifted because there is not enough length. Blouse styles that have gathers or pleats from the neckline, shoulder line or from a high yoke accommodate the kyphosis best, but although inverted pleats at the centre back provide extra room they will also gape (Figs. 40a and 40b).

A blouse and skirt would solve the hemline problem for women, as the hump will only affect the length of the blouse, and this will be hidden by the skirt. Even better, a blouse and skirt in the same fabric will look like a dress. The best solution to the problem, however, is to make or have made your own blouses, skirts, jackets or shirts. Figs. 69 and 70 on p. 93 explain how patterns may be adapted. Fig. 41 shows an outfit made to hang straight. Fig. 42 shows the dress laid flat.

42 Garment flat (kyphosis)

43 Garment being worn (scoliosis)

44 Alternative garments (scoliosis)

Scoliosis

A twist of the spine creates an asymmetrical figure, somewhat S-shaped, which is shorter from the armhole to the waist on one side, and longer from the waistline to the hem on the same side as it passes over the protruding hip. The waist is, therefore, at an angle. Fitted garments collect in folds at waist level on one side, and the hemline swings to one side. Our aim is to camouflage the angle of the waist, and bring the eye either upwards towards the face or downwards to the seat or hem. Fig. 43 has a pin-tucked yoke and pretty collar. Fig. 44 shows a skirt shaped round the hip and a waistcoat. A dress with a yoke or pleated from the shoulder will hang straighter. Waisted styles only emphasize the problem. Alternatively, a blouson style top or long jumper bypasses the waistline and skirts and trousers can be made to hang straight.

Wheelchairs

People confined to wheelchairs come in all shapes and sizes, and can be wheelchair-bound for many different reasons. Sitting down for long periods creates clothing problems. More fabric is needed around the back to keep the waistband in the correct place, and less fabric is required in front to eliminate the folds which form. With a ready-made skirt or pair of trousers the front can be lowered to give a better appearance. You can also alter a pattern by lowering the front, but it can be extended at the back too. In addition, trouser patterns can be lengthened, shortened, made wider or narrower to meet individual needs (Fig. 45).

Many people who are wheelchair-bound find there is too much fabric between the back neck and the waist, so a fold or crease forms across the back at approximately mid armhole. This can be folded and pinned out either on the pattern or on the ready-made blouse, skirt, or dress, which then creates a neat back yoke.

If you have become round shouldered you

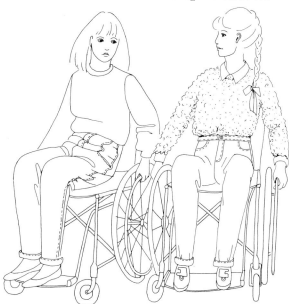

45 Trousers for wheelchairs

may find the back neck of the garment stands away from your neck and catches in your hair when you move. Extra fabric can be eliminated by either shaping the back seam to fit the curve to the neck, or by putting in neck darts. It is easier to alter a neckline without a collar if this is the problem. Propelling a wheelchair develops arm and chest muscles. Often sleeves do not give sufficient room around the top of the arms. It is best to look for the wider armhole types of sleeve as shown in Fig. 34 on p. 54. Sometimes garments bought to fit the chest size can be too big on the shoulders and around the neck. Styles with pleats from the shoulders or from a yoke give more room but fit reasonably well elsewhere. Pleats or gathers across the back help to ease movement when propelling the chair and take the strain away from sleeve seams.

Women who prefer a three-quarter sleeve or a long shirt style with a cuff find that too much fullness is not advisable as the fabric trails on the wheels. Equally, a defined waistline is not always a good idea for a wheelchair user. It emphasizes the difference in size and proportion between the two halves of the body. Skirts or trousers with

46a Suit for a person in a wheelchair

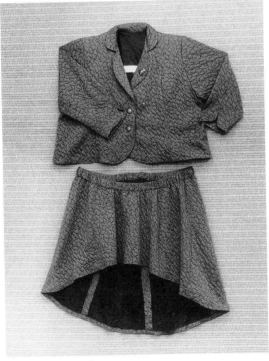

46b Garment flat

blouson-style tops look best, while for men waistcoats can take the eye away from the waist. Jackets tend to pull on the bottom button, and also concertina. They can be shaped so that they come to the lap at the front but remain full length at the back. Dresses with a yoke do not have to look like a tent, but can be flared or pleated into the yoke to give the required amount of width. All garments shaped to suit a seated figure are for people who have to sit all the time. They would look strange on a standing figure (Figs. 46a and 46b).

Arthritis

Problems for arthritis sufferers are mainly manipulative, but many people also lean forward from the hips when walking, and this will lift the back hemline and lower the front. If there is sufficient fabric length at the back the garment can be lifted at the front waist until it hangs straight. This alteration can also be made to skirts or dresses with a basque or hip yoke. Elevated shoulders shorten the appearance of the neck, so the choice of neckline is important see Figs. 13, 14 and 15 on pp. 23–4. Enlarged knee joints require straight-legged trousers. Instructions for widening a trouser leg are given on p. 84 (see Fig. 56a).

Restricted growth

Here there are two problem areas to consider. First, people who are short in stature but whose bodies are in proportion, and second, people who have a standard body size but who have very short arms and legs.

The major problem for the first group is to buy clothing suitable for their age. Nowadays, children's styles tend to mirror those of their parents, so finding separates and leisure-wear is not too difficult, but problems arise when more formal wear is required. The smallest size available in a man's suit at a standard chain tailors/outfitters is 71 cm (28 in.) waist, 87 cm (34 in.) chest, while

Young's Dress Hire stock a suit size 66 cm (26 in.) waist, 81 cm (32 in.) chest. Patterns for men's suits usually start at 92 cm (36 in.) chest, but some patterns are available for unisex jackets at 71–76 cm (28–30 in.), and 81–87 cm (32–34 in). Patterns for women's suits usually start at size 8, but some pattern companies do have a size 6.

The second group can have tremendous problems. All garments are too long in the sleeve, or too long from the waist. Trousers bought to fit the hip size will need the legs shortened and re-shaped and could also need alterations to the depth between waist and crotch. It is far easier to adapt a pattern than alter ready-made trousers. Then, trouser legs can be made straight and reasonably loose to balance the body weight. Getting on or off a seat built for people with longer legs can be quite a problem and can put a lot of strain on a garment. Often a style with an elasticated waist band gives a better grip around the waist. Pocket positions on all garments should be positioned so that the wearer can reach and make use of them.

Jackets will need the sleeves shortened above and below the elbow to keep the elbow shaping correct. This is an enormous task on a tailored jacket. Extra width may be needed around the top of the arm, and this is often difficult to find in a ready-made garment. Here again it is easier, and the result more satisfying, if you buy a pattern and adapt it to your own shape and requirements. A semi-fitted, single-breasted jacket would be the most flattering style for men or women, but women can also wear a simple edge-to-edge, Chanel-style jacket. Finally, the jacket length needs to be carefully considered. A slightly shorter jacket will appear to lengthen the legs, but the best method is to stand in front of a mirror and see which length suits you best.

Should any of the ideas given in this chapter solve your particular problem the following chapters will explain the alterations and adaptations in more detail.

6 SEWING WITH A DISABILITY

Sewing can be an ideal occupation for a person with a disability. It can be done at home with a minimum of equipment and a little help from parents and friends, at a Day Centre, where equipment will be provided, or at a day or evening Further Education class. There are a few training centres specially set up to help disabled people and their relatives learn to design and make patterns and garments specifically for themselves. Those centres will also train professional carers and teachers of Dress and Home Economics how to adapt their own skills to accommodate the clothing needs of disabled people.

If you haven't sewn before, or if you are working with a disabled person, it is necessary to examine each stage of the sewing process and find out where difficulties might arise. Together you should be able to find a way of overcoming them. Special gadgets can be expensive, but sometimes a little ingenuity is all that is needed. For example, if sewing a straight line is a problem for a

47 Helping the disabled to sew

visually impaired person try sticking a pencil or a piece of thick card to the machine the distance of a seam allowance away from the needle. If the edge of the fabric abuts the edge of the card the seam will be the correct width and the stitching will be straight. A specially extended quilting guide would do a similar job (see fig. 48).

There will always be some people who are very limited in what they are able to do but who, nevertheless, would like to be involved in choosing, designing and making their own clothes. A helper can draw to their directions, steer the fabric through the machine while they use the controls, and show how a garment is assembled by explaining to them each process as it is done. With a little encouragement many disabled people can do far more than they imagine, and can derive a great deal of pleasure and satisfaction from their involvement (Fig. 47). A young lady I worked with who could not use her hands or move her arms made a garment by doing the hand sewing with her teeth and enlisted the help of a friend to use the machine. She worked the controls with her chin while her friend guided the fabric.

Equipment

All that is needed to start sewing is a table, a pair of sharp scissors, pins, needle and thread, a tape-measure and possibly a sewing machine if it is availabe. Once enthusiasm takes hold, you can add to the 'tools'. To help, a complete list of equipment follows. Most things are reasonably cheap and they do make sewing easier.

A good-sized table. Check that it is at a convenient height for the user. A normal table height could be much too high for a small person in a wheelchair.

Tape-measure. Choose a good quality tape with metric and imperial markings.

Ruler in clear plastic.

1-metre rule for pattern making and alterations.

Sewing gauge to mark seam and hem allowances and plan buttonholes. A piece of card specially cut can do the same job.

Tracing wheel and dressmakers' carbon. When the carbon paper is placed between the fabric and the pattern the pattern markings can be traced quickly and accurately on to the fabric.

Tailors' chalk. Used for marking hemlines and alterations, etc. Also useful to mark a sewing line for anyone who finds sewing a straight seam difficult.

Pencil to alter patterns.

Pins. Pins with coloured heads are easier to see, feel and hold.

Pincushion to keep unused pins safe.

Paper scissors to cut patterns – paper blunts dressmaking scissors.

Sticky tape or glue for pattern enlargement.

Dressmaking scissors to cut fabric.

Stitch ripper to unpick stitching and cut buttonholes. To be used with care!

Embroidery scissors. Useful for trimming and snipping.

Electric scissors can make cutting easier for some people. Others cannot stand the vibration.

Needles. Many disabled people find a crewel needle much easier to thread and hold because it is a long needle with a large eye. Sizes of most hand-sewing needles range from 3 to 12, 3 being the heavier and 12 the finer needle. A fine needle is needed for very lightweight fabrics. If you only have the use of one hand it is easier to put the needle into a pincushion before threading. Some people prefer needle-threaders, while others may use the calyx-eyed needle which has an opening at the top.

Thimble

Machine needles. These need to be the correct thickness and type for the fabric to

67

be used. Sizes range from the finer 9 (65) to the thicker 18 (110) needle, the reverse of hand-sewing needles. Ballpoint needles are better for knitted fabrics because their rounded tip does not damage the fibres and cause runs. Special needles are also available for jeans and leather. It is wise to make sure the needle is inserted correctly, and to make frequent checks to see that the needle has not blunted or bent. Blunt or faulty needles will cause problems with stitching.

Sewing machines. People with a disability vary widely in their manipulative skills, so no one sewing machine is better than another. The choice of sewing machine is dependent upon the needs and the means of the individual. A person with jerky arm movements may find that a hand machine controls the jerks once the handle is gripped.

People in wheelchairs need a machine which threads at the front and has dials and instructions facing them. Most people who use an electric sewing machine appreciate a variable speed control. A finger guard to attach to the machine is also a valuable piece of equipment. Those unable to use a foot control can often work it by hand or elbow if it is placed on the table. If they have limited ability to press, the Elna Air Electronic control is excellent, because it is small with a rubber centre and is very light. It can be used in the hand, on the knee, on the table or on the machine itself, where one finger can work the control while the remainder are free to help guide the fabric. Each person will find the best position for him or her. (Fig. 48).

Computerized machines are valuable to those people who can exert no pressure, as at the touch of a button the machine is pro-

48 Elna sewing machines

grammed to any one of a number of fancy stitches, to embroider names or motifs, or make buttonholes all the same size.

Thread. Used for tacking and sewing. It is never advisable to tack a light-coloured garment with dark sewing thread as points of colour may be left when the threads are removed.

Plain pattern paper. Thin, strong paper for making or altering patterns.

Calico/an old sheet/curtain lining to make a personal pattern.

Full-length mirror to check fit and appearance.

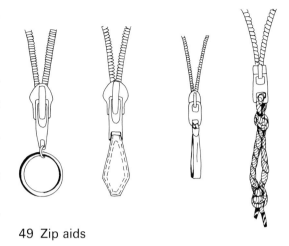

49 Zip aids

Fastenings

If you work with a number of disabled people you may find it useful to make a tabard which has on it a selection of fastenings of varying shapes and sizes. This can be used as a test garment which each person puts on to determine the type and size of fastenings he or she can manage unaided. A good fastening is one that helps a disabled person to be more independent and is sympathetic to the garment, without creating other problems.

Zips

Long back zips are impossible for most disabled people and for many elderly people as well. You need to be very supple to manage a long zip. A shorter, 10–12 cm (4–5 in.) zip at the back of the neck may be much easier. Back zips are of value for people who are unable to dress themselves, as they can put their arms into the garment from the front. However it must be a fine, flat, nylon zip to prevent pressure sores. There are zips on the market that show no teeth at the back at all when closed. It is always wise to check that the skin is not caught in a metal zip and that the top of the zip does not dig into the neck, because this could go unnoticed if the person being dressed is paralyzed or has communication problems.

Trouser zips are often too short, but can be replaced easily by a slightly longer zip. While open-ended zips can be difficult to grip and fasten, closed front zips can be managed by most people, especially if a ring, tab or loop is attached to the slide. These can be decorative as well as functional (Fig. 49).

Buttons

Usually, small buttons are difficult for disabled people to manage, so it is best to try different sizes and shapes. For some people square buttons prove easier than round, dome buttons better than flat. Certainly toggle fastenings are easier to grasp and can be very suitable for casual-style garments. Fabric- or leather-covered buttons do not slip easily through buttonholes and are not advisable.

Hooks

As with buttons, small hooks are hard to see, feel, and hold. Large trouser hooks and bars are the easiest to handle and suitable for waistbands, but most hooks prove difficult for people with manipulative problems.

Press studs

Press studs can be difficult for people who have the use of only one hand, because you need a hard surface underneath to push against. This means a press stud is easy to fasten against a bone but much more difficult against softer parts of the body. Small press studs are difficult for those with a poor grasp or lack of co-ordination, and they are not suitable in places where there is likely to be tension, for example the front fastening on a fitted garment whose wearer manoeuvers his or her own wheelchair.

Laces

Shoelaces are difficult for children with clumsy fingers, people with only one hand or with manipulative problems, and they can be difficult to reach if the person is arthritic or in a wheelchair. However, elastic laces are now available which enables shoes to be put on without being unfastened.

Tapes

The ends of tapes can become caught in wheels and doors where they are easily torn off. They are also difficult to untie when knotted or wet.

Velcro

Velcro is much more effective and accurate when used in small pieces, for example circular Velcro spot-ons. Fluff will catch in large areas of Velcro and render it ineffective. Consequently, Velcro should always be fastened before washing. The looped side can also catch on other clothing and cause snags. Having said this, Velcro enables many disabled people to be independent, as it is the only fastening they can manage. It also lies flat and does not create pressure sores.

Buckles

Buckles can give a firm and decorative fastening and often they can be fastened with one hand. However, it is wise to check that the prongs lie flat and do not cause any discomfort.

7 MEASUREMENTS

If we were to take the measurements of a large number of people it is unlikely that very many would be 'standard sizes'. All women know how uncomfortable they feel in a skirt whose waist is too tight or in the wrong place, or in a dress where the skirt rides up and seems to be a size smaller than the top. Sometimes shoulder seams are too wide or not wide enough, and bust darts create space where it's not wanted, or take away fabric where it is needed!

If these are problems we all experience, what chance do disabled people have of finding garments that fit and hang correctly, are comfortable to wear, and meet their individual needs? Often they have to buy garments larger than their size to enable them to get dressed more easily, and then they find that the sleeves are too long, the waist is too low, and the length is wrong. When all the alterations have been made the balance of the garment has changed and so it still looks wrong. Disabled people who are wheelchair-bound often find that trouser waistbands are too low at the back and too high at the front. They have a collection of fabric at the front crotch which makes fastening the zip difficult. Skirts also have unnecessary fabric at the front, so the front hemline dips but who knows where the back ends up!

To be comfortable and to look good the garment needs to follow the shape of the person wearing it. Our bodies are a different shape in a sitting position than when standing. It is important that the body is measured in the position in which it will be when the garment is worn. Should the person sit for most of the time but walk occasionally, it would be wise to take both sitting and standing measurements to ensure maximum comfort in the finished skirt or trousers. Never be tempted to lay the person on the bed or on the floor to take measurements because it makes life easier for you. The body weight is distributed differently once in the wheelchair, and any garment made to those measurements would not fit.

Disabled people look far less disabled in clothes made to accommodate their shape than they do in clothes made to standard measurements, but the garments will be a non-standard shape when taken off. Some people will not mind this because to them it is more important to look good when they wear the garments, but others cannot accept clothes that look different to those of their peer group. Anyone involved in making clothes for the disabled needs to check this point before measuring and making patterns. Many disabled people will need reassurance that the end result will be a garment they are happy to wear because it does look exactly like those of their peers when it is worn (Figs. 50a and 50b).

Taking Measurements

Measuring someone in a wheelchair can be very difficult. The person doing the measuring may need help in moving or holding the person being measured, so make sure someone is available to help before you start. The

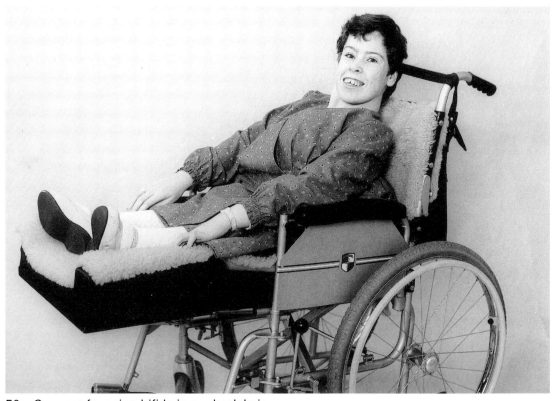

50a Garment for spina bifida in a wheelchair

50b Garment flat

sides of a wheechair are usually removeable. Take off one side at a time and check that the disabled person still feels safe and supported, because any securing belts may need to be undone as well. For the measurements up to the back waist it is easier to pass the tape-measure through the back of the wheelchair and measure up to the waist. If moving is difficult the back waist, under the bottom to the foot-rest can be done from the side. The outside leg measurement is from the side waist, over the hip and down to the level of the crease between leg and bottom, then to the side, and on to the foot-rest, following what will be the side seam of the trousers (Fig. 51).

People who can stand to be measured should stand in a safe position holding a zimmer, rail, or chair back, and should be encouraged to inform you when they need a rest. You must ensure that the person being measured is not making an effort to stand or sit straight while you measure them. They

51 Measuring outside leg

need to be measured in their 'normal' position.

The following tips apply when measuring people of all shapes and sizes: Take all measurements with two fingers inside the tape-measure to give a little extra ease (Fig.

52). Measure the figure over the undergarments and appliances that normally would be worn under the finished garment. Start by tying a piece of narrow elastic or string around the waist and allow it to find the natural waistline, or the place where clothing will rest. For example, someone with a spinal lesion at waist level will find that skirts and trousers will settle above or below the rounded deformity. It is best to check with the wearer which position is most comfortable. You will find this elastic useful to measure to and from. Take separate measurements for right and left sides where sides differ.

Dresses, blouses, or shirts (Fig. 53 a)

1 Around the neck – drop the tape down to the top of the two bones at the front of the neck.
2 Around the bust/chest – measure at the fullest part of the bust/chest and slightly up at the back. If the tape is allowed to drop, the resulting measurement could be too tight.
3 Around the waist – where the string has settled.

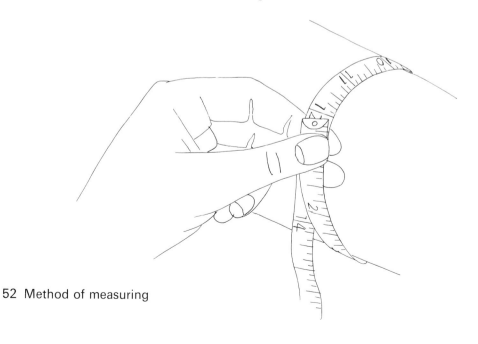

52 Method of measuring

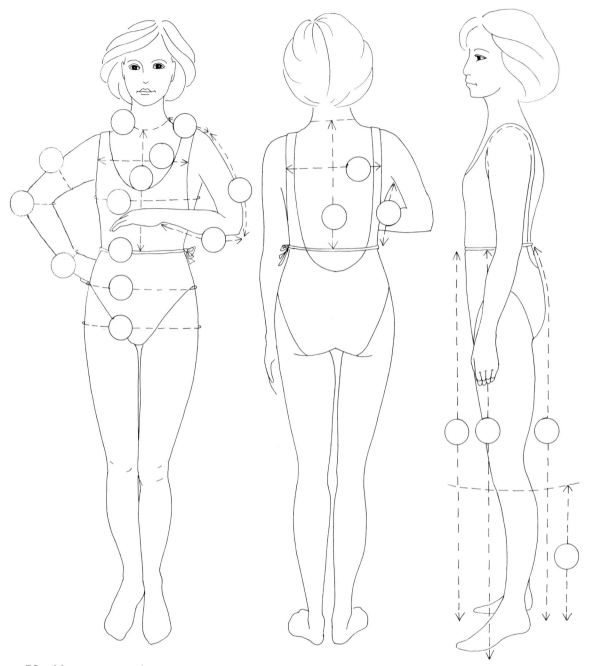

53a Measurement charts

4 Around the high hip – at the level of the hip bone. Make a note of the distance down from the waist.

5 Around the hips – at the fullest part of the hips, usually over the bottom. Make a note of the distance down from the waist.

6 Across the upper chest – armhole to armhole about 10 cm (4 in.) below the base of the throat, or just before the armhole starts to curve under the arm.

7 Across the upper back – armhole to armhole about 13 cm (5 in.) below the top bone in the spine, or before the armhole starts to curve under the arm. In some cases it may be necessary to record a right and left side, from the left side to the spine, and from the spine to the right side. If the person propels his or her own wheelchair, or walks with a zimmer, take this measurement with the arms forward.

8 Back neck to waist – from the nape of the neck to the waistline.

9 Front neck to waist – from the base of the throat to the waistline.

10 Underarm to waist – both right and left sides.

11 Length of shoulder – from the side neck to the top of the shoulder, right and left.

12 Top of the shoulder to the wrist bone, above little finger – right and left.

14 Around the upper arm – taken at the fullest part. Right and left.

15 Around the elbow – with the arm bent. Right and left.

16 Around the wrist – taken over the wrist bone. Right and left.

17 Scye circumference – around the armhole with the arm in a natural position. Right and left.

18 Back waist to floor (or foot rest). Follow the body line if seated.

19 Front waist to floor (or foot rest). Follow the body line if seated.

20 Side waist to floor (or foot rest). Right and left sides. Follow the body line if seated.

21 The required length of the garment from the floor or foot-rest.

Measurements for blouses or shirts finish at No. 17.

Skirts

3 Waist – as for dresses.
4 High hip – as for dresses.
5 Hip – as for dresses.
18 Back waist to floor (or foot-rest) – as for dresses.
19 Front waist to floor (or foot-rest) – as for dresses.
20 Side waist to floor (or foot-rest) – as for dresses.
21 Required length of garment from floor (or foot-rest) – as for dresses.

Trousers (Fig. 53b)

3 Waist – as for dresses.
4 High hip – as for dresses.
5 Hip (seat) – as for dresses.
22 Around the thigh – at the widest part. Right and left legs.
23 Around the knee – right and left.
24 Around the ankle – right and left.
25 The outside leg – from the waist over the hips to the floor; both right and left sides. If seated follow the side seam on the trousers being worn, or measure from the waist, over the hips to the place where the hip joint meets the leg, along the side of the leg to the knee, and down to the foot-rest; both right and left sides.
26 The inside leg – from the crotch to the floor or foot-rest; both right and left sides.

Trouser widths and lengths will change with fashion, and a decision can be made at this stage as to how far from the floor or foot-rest the trouser hem needs to be.

27 The body rise – from the side waist, over the hips to the seat of the chair; both right and left sides. With wheelchair users, check that you measure to the depressed part of the cushion where the body rests, not to the top of the cushion.

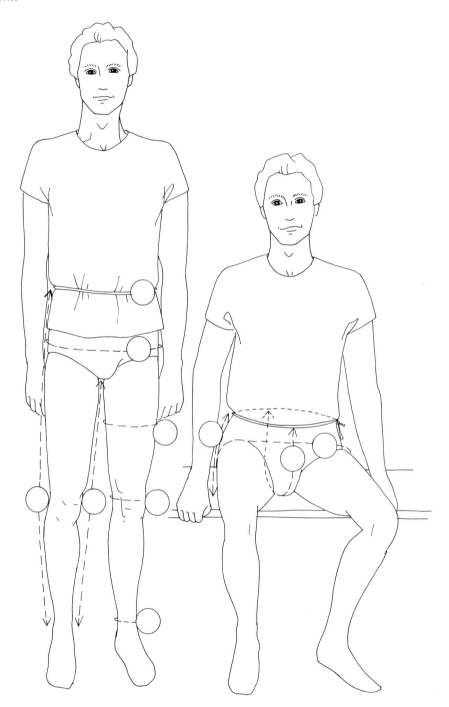

53b Measurement charts

28 The crotch length – from the centre back waist, through the legs to the centre front waist. It is a good idea to take this measurement when trousers are being worn. Make a note independently of the measurement from centre back waist to the crotch seam, and from the centre front waist to the crotch seam. While the overall measurement should remain the same whether sitting or standing, the distance to the crotch seam will vary between front and back.

Foundation garments: bra

To buy a bra to your correct size measure round the body under the bust. If the measurement is an even number add 10 cm (4 in.); if odd add 13 cm (5 in.). The total number is your *bra size*. For example, measurement under bust is 86 cm (34 in.) + 10 cm (4 in.) = 96 cm (38 in.). *Bra size* is 96 cm (38 in.).

Now measure the bust at the fullest part. The cup size depends on the difference between the bust measurement and the bra size. If the measurement is the same as your bra size you need an A cup; 2.5 cm (1 in.) more a B cup; 5 cm (2 in.) more a C cup; 8 cm (3 in.) more a D cup; 10 cm (4 in.) more a DD cup; 13 cm (5 in.) more an E cup; 15 cm (6 in.) more an F cup. For example, bust measurement is 100 cm ($39\frac{1}{2}$ in.). Bra size is 96 cm (38 in.). Difference is 100 cm ($39\frac{1}{2}$ in.) – 96 cm (38 in.) = 4 cm (2 in.) = C cup. Therefore you would buy a 96 cm (38 in.) C cup bra. Bra size can alter according to age, diet and exercise.

Buying a Pattern

Choosing a pattern can be fun. It doesn't matter if you can't get to a shop and browse through pattern books, because smaller, more manageable books are available at regular intervals from the newsagent. These will keep you up to date with fashions and ideas. The books have order forms, but you may prefer to get someone to buy the pattern for you locally, once you have made your choice. Patterns are divided into a number of different categories related to height and figure type. If you look at the back of the pattern book you will see all the different groups listed with their sizes and measurements. Should you not have a book, the categories are listed here, but not every pattern manufacturer makes the full range.

Babies *(who are not yet walking)*

Age	Newborn (1–3 months)	6 months
Weight	3–6 kg ($6\frac{1}{2}$–13 lb)	6–8 kg (13–17 lb)
Height	43–61 cm (17–24 in.)	61–67 cm (24–26 in.)

Toddlers *(where an allowance is made for nappies)*

Size	$\frac{1}{2}$	1	2	3	4	
Breast or chest	48	51	53	56	58	cm
Waist	48	50	51	52	53	cm
Finished dress length	35.5	38	40.5	43	46	cm
Approx. height	71	79	87	94	102	cm
	28	31	$34\frac{1}{4}$	37	$40\frac{1}{4}$	in.

Children

Size	2	3	4	5	6	6x	
Breast or chest	53	56	58	61	64	65	cm
Waist	51	52	53	55	56	57	cm
Hip	–	–	61	64	66	67	cm
Back waist length	22	23	24	25.5	27	27.5	cm
Finished dress length	46	48	51	56	61	64	cm
Approx. height	89	97	104	112	119	122	cm
	35	38	41	44	47	48	in

Measurements

Girls *(who have not yet begun to mature)*

Size	7	8	10	12	14	
Breast	66	69	73	76	81	cm
Waist	58	60	62	65	67	cm
Hip	69	71	76	81	87	cm
Back waist length	29.5	31	32.5	34.5	36	cm
Approx. height	127	132	142	149	155	cm
		50	52	56	59	61 in.

Chubby *(for growing girls over average weight for their age and height)*

Size	$8\frac{1}{2}c$	$10\frac{1}{2}c$	$12\frac{1}{2}c$	$14\frac{1}{2}c$	
Breast	76	80	84	88	cm
Waist	71	74	76	79	cm
Hip	84	88	92	96	cm
Back waist length	32	34	35.5	37.5	cm
Approx. height	132	142	149	155	cm
	52	56	59	61 in.	

Young Junior/Teens
(for developing pre-teen and teenage figures)
Height without shoes 1.55 m (5 ft 1 in.) to 1.6 m (5 ft 3 in.)

Size	5/6	7/8	9/10	11/12	13/14	15/16	
Bust	71	74	78	81	85	89	cm
Waist	56	58	61	64	66	69	cm
Hip	79	81	85	89	93	97	cm
Back waist length	34.5	35.5	37	38	39	40	cm

Junior Petite
(for a well-proportioned, small figure)
Height without shoes 1.52 m (5 ft) to 1.55 m (5 ft 1 in.)

Size	3jp	5jp	7jp	9jp	11jp	13jp	
Bust	76	79	81	84	87	89	cm
Waist	56	58	61	64	66	69	cm
Hip	79	81	84	87	89	92	cm
Back waist length	35.5	36	37	37.5	38	39	cm

Junior
(for a well-proportioned, shorter, waisted figure)
Height without shoes 1.63 m (5 ft 4in.) to 1.65 m (5 ft 5 in.)

Size	5	7	9	11	13	15	
Bust	76	79	81	85	89	94	cm
Waist	57	60	62	65	69	74	cm
Hip	81	84	87	90	94	99	cm
Back waist length	38	39	39.5	40	40.5	41.5	cm

Misses
(for a well-proportioned and developed figure)
Height without shoes 1.65 m (5 ft 5in.) to 1.68 m (5 ft 6 in.)

Size	6	8	10	12	14	16	18	20	22	24	
Bust	78	80	83	87	92	97	102	107	112	117	cm
Waist	58	61	64	67	71	76	81	87	94	99	cm
Hip	83	85	88	92	97	102	107	112	117	122	cm
Back waist length	39.5	40	40.5	41.5	42	42.5	43	44	44	44.5	cm

Miss Petite
(for the shorter figure)
Height without shoes 1.57 m (5 ft 2in.) to 1.63 m (5 ft 4 in.)

Size	6mp	8mp	10mp	12mp	14mp	16mp	
Bust	78	80	83	87	92	97	cm
Waist	60	62	65	69	73	78	cm
Hip	83	85	88	92	97	102	cm
Back waist length	37	37.5	38	39	39.5	40	cm

Women

(for the larger, more mature figure)
Height without shoes 1.65 m (5 ft 5in.) to 1.68 m
(5 ft 6 in.)

Size	38	40	42	44	46	48	50
Bust	107	112	117	122	127	132	137 cm
Waist	89	94	99	105	112	118	124 cm
Hip	112	117	122	127	132	137	142 cm
Back waist length	44	44	44.5	45	45	45.5	46 cm

Half size

(for a fully developed figure with a short back neck to waist measurement)
Height without shoes 1.51 m (5 ft 1in.) to 1.60 m
(5 ft 2 in.)

Size	$10\frac{1}{2}$	$12\frac{1}{2}$	$14\frac{1}{2}$	$16\frac{1}{2}$	$18\frac{1}{2}$	$20\frac{1}{2}$	$22\frac{1}{2}$	$24\frac{1}{2}$
Bust	84	89	94	99	104	109	114	119 cm
Waist	69	74	79	84	89	96	102	108 cm
Hip	89	94	99	104	109	116	122	128 cm
Back waist length	38	39	39.5	40	40.5	40.5	41	41.5 cm

To decide which is the correct pattern size for you, you need to check your measurements against the chart which best describes your figure style. Choosing well at this stage could save a lot of work later. For a dress, blouse, jacket or coat pattern, buy the correct bust size, and for a skirt or trousers, the hip size. For men, a shirt pattern is bought by the collar size, trousers by the hip size, and a jacket or coat by the chest size.

Boys and teen boys

(for growing boys and young men)

Size	BOYS				TEEN-BOYS			
	7	8	10	12	14	16	18	20
Chest	66	69	71	76	81	85	89	93 cm
Waist	58	61	64	66	69	71	74	76 cm
Hip (seat)	69	71	75	79	83	87	90	94 cm
Neckband	30	31	32	33	34.5	35.5	37	38 cm
Height	122	127	137	147	155	163	168	173 cm
Shirt sleeve	57	59	64	68	74	76	79	81 cm

Men

(of average build)
Height without shoes about 1.78 m (5 ft 10 in.)

Size	34	36	38	40	42	44	46	48
Chest	87	92	97	102	107	112	117	122 cm
Waist	71	76	81	87	92	99	107	112 cm
Hip (seat)	89	94	99	104	109	114	119	124 cm
Neckband	35.5	37	38	39.5	40.5	42	43	44.5 cm
Shirt sleeve	81	81	84	84	87	87	89	89 cm

It is beneficial to make yourself a measurement chart detailing your own measurements which are relevant to the garment you wish to make. Alongside your measurements write down the ones given for your size on the pattern envelope. Remember that 'round' measurements have the necessary ease allowed for the style you have chosen, and should measure more than your bust, chest, or hip measurement. All other measurements not detailed on the envelope need to be checked on the pattern itself, and

Personal Measurement Chart

	My Measurements	Pattern Measurements	Difference
*Bust/chest	92 cm (36 in.)	92 cm (36 in.)	
*Waist	76 cm (30 in.)	71 cm (28 in.)	+ 5 cm (2 in.)
*Hips	102 cm (40 in.)	97 cm (38 in.)	+ 5 cm (2 in.)
*Back neck to waist	37 cm ($14\frac{1}{2}$ in.)	42 cm ($16\frac{1}{2}$ in.)	− 5 cm (2 in.)
Add other appropriate measurements as suggested in the previous section: for example, length of shoulder. *From pattern envelope.			

should be taken between the stitching lines. The complete chart will enable you to see at a glance where alterations need to be made. When using a pattern for the first time cut the pattern pieces out roughly, leaving space around the cutting lines for any necessary alterations. Press them flat with a warm, dry iron before checking the measurements. Measure around curves with your tape-measure on its edge, or with a piece of string, measuring the string once the length has been determined. If a bodice pattern has darts hold the pattern piece against you in its correct position, and mark on the pattern where the point of the bust lies. Multi-sized patterns enable you to flit from one size to another to accommodate or dispose of extra width. 'Personalized instructions' written on the front of the pattern envelope indicates that it gives detailed information on fitting.

If your figure is symmetrical most alterations can be made to the pattern by adding or removing width or length. If, however, your figure is assymmetrical it is advisable to do any alterations you can on the paper pattern and then cut out the pattern from an old sheet, curtain lining, or calico. It is easier to check the fit and hang of the garment on this 'toile', and make any further adjustments, before you cut into expensive fabric.

8 PATTERN ALTERATIONS

Altering a pattern can be a relatively easy process, provided that you have chosen to start with a simple style that has few pattern pieces. A large number of pieces is confusing and makes alterations difficult. A simple style, or a basic or 'shell' pattern, consists of a simple bodice, a sleeve and plain skirt, or a trouser back and front with waistband. It can be useful to start with this kind of pattern because it enables you to get the correct body shape, and it often indicates the kind of style that will suit you best.

When patterns only need lengthening, shortening, or a little width added or subtracted, each pattern piece will have a line showing you where to make the alteration. It is an easy process to adjust the pattern and then cut it out in the fabric of your choice. For an asymmetrical figure, someone who is wheechair-bound, or for anyone who lacks the confidence to tackle more substantial alterations, this chapter will describe, step by step, how they should be done.

To check that the alterations work, cut the pattern out from an old sheet or calico material and make up the garment on the machine using a long stitch. This trial garment, or 'toile', is much easier to fit than a paper pattern, but don't use tacking stitches, as they have a nasty habit of coming undone during the fitting! The trial garment will show you what further alterations may be needed. These can be pinned out or fabric let in, and the toile may also be marked to show fitting lines at the neck and sleeve, and skirt or trouser lengths. When you are happy that the toile fits correctly, check with the person

wearing it that it is comfortable to sit in, that it gives sufficient room to allow easy movement when wheeling or walking, and that it will accommodate any appliances.

Once the garment fits satisfactorily, transfer any alterations you have made back onto the paper pattern. From this, if you wish, you can cut a master pattern in a medium-weight, sew-in Vilene, and use it many times without tearing. All this may seem a long drawn-out process when you are itching to get your scissors into fabric and see the garment made up. However, if a little time is spent at this stage both you and the wearer will be happier and more satisfied with the end result.

Making a Trial Garment, or 'Toile'

The aim is to produce a garment which hangs correctly, has a straight hemline, looks good and is comfortable to wear. Once you have bought a pattern to your correct size and figure type you need to check the rest of your measurements and record them on your personal measurement chart. Bust, chest, waist, hips and back neck to waist measurements are checked agaisnt the pattern envelope, not measured. Other measurements are checked by measuring the pattern pieces with a tape-measure between the stitching lines, not counting the seam allowances.

When measuring the sleeve length, note where the elbow comes if the sleeve is a fitted style. If bust darts are involved hold the pattern against you in the correct position and mark where the bust lies. Does the dart point in that direction or does it need to be higher or lower? Check the width of the sleeve at the widest part underarm, at the elbow and at the wrist. Check trouser width at the thigh, knee and ankle. The amount of room required in sleeves and trouser legs will depend on fashion, life-style and any appliances worn. Make your tape-measure into a circle measuring the width of the pattern and slot it over the arm or leg in the correct position to make sure there is room to move within that measurement and that it is a satisfactory width for the style.

Once the measurements have been checked and recorded you can proceed with the basic alterations to the paper pattern. Alterations to skirts and trousers for asymmetrical or sitting figures also need to be made at this stage, as it is extremely difficult to slash a garment and let pieces in when someone is sitting on it!

When the trial garment is cut out mark clearly across each piece where the bust or chest, waist, hip, seat and knee lines are, also the centre back and centre front vertical lines and any bodice darts to the bust and from the waist. Make up the garment showing these markings on the outside. Leave the waist darts to be fitted on the body. For skirts and trousers, the seam allowance can be folded over at the waist and stitched down close to the raw edge. A string or tape slotted through will hold the waist in position for fitting.

Altering a Trouser Pattern

Decide how far from the floor or foot-rest you would like your trouser hem to be and subtract this from your inside and outside leg measurements. This will tell you how long the trouser pattern needs to be, excluding seam allowances. Positions for shortening and lengthening patterns are marked on the pattern paper. To guide you when making alterations, other useful lines have been marked on Fig. 54a.

To shorten the trouser leg (Fig. 54b)

1 From the lengthen/shorten line measure up the amount that needs to be removed and mark at each side of the leg.
2 Fold the pattern along the lengthen/shorten line and take the fold up to the marks you have made. Secure with pins.
3 If necessary, redraw the side seam to give a smooth line.
4 Fold out the same amount on the back pattern.

To lengthen the trouser leg (Fig. 54c)

1 Cut across the pattern at the lengthen/shorten line on both back and front patterns.
2 Place a piece of paper behind the pattern, then separate the two pattern pieces until the measurement between them is equal to the amount by which the trousers need to be lengthened.
3 Secure with pins. Redraw side seams, and cut excess paper away.

To alter the length from waist to crotch (Crotch Depth)

On the lengthen/shorten line indicated on the pattern, fold out or let in the amount necessary to give your correct crotch depth measurement.

To shorten the back seam, waist to crotch (Fig. 55a)

1 Check the back waist to crotch measurement on the pattern against your own measurement. The difference is the amount to be removed.
2 Measure down the centre back seam,

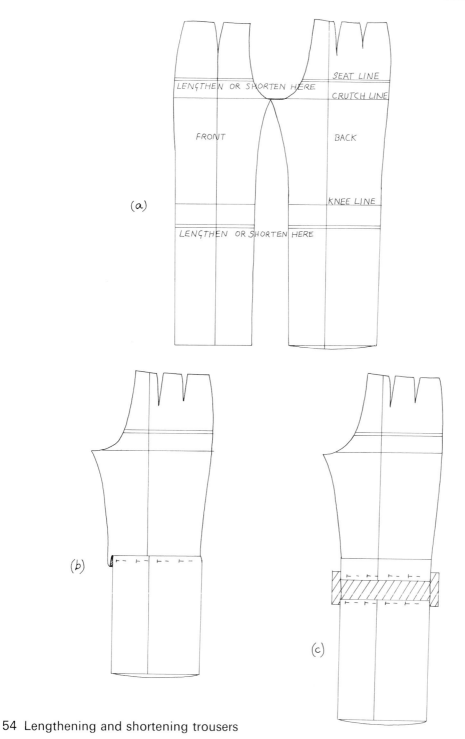

54 Lengthening and shortening trousers

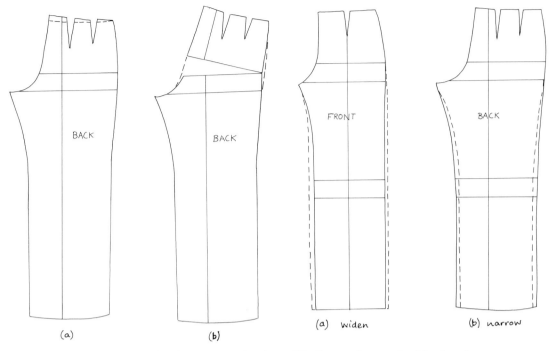

55 Shortening and lengthening trouser back

56 Narrowing and widening legs

from the waist, the amount to be removed.

3 Draw a new line from this point to the side seam.

To lengthen the back seam, waist to crotch (Fig. 55b)

1 Cut along the seat line from the centre back seam, stopping at the stitching line.
2 Open the back seam the required amount and re-shape the back and side seam lines.

Widening or narrowing trouser legs (Fig. 56a and 56b)

As fashions change you may need to add or subtract width to or from the trouser legs. This is done in equal amounts at the inside and outside leg, on both front and back patterns.

1 Mark at knee level one-quarter of the amount by which you wish to widen or narrow the legs.

2 Starting at the trouser fork, draw a new curve down to the knee point, then keeping the same distance away from the original line continue down to the hemline.

57 Large tummy alteration

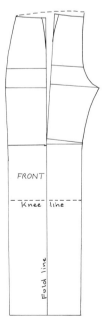

To accommodate a large tummy (Fig. 57)

Draw a line across the front pattern about half way between crotch and knee line. Fold the trouser leg in half, lengthwise, and mark the fold. Cut down this fold from the waistline to the line you have drawn, then along the new line to the inside seam. Move the front section forwards and downwards, opening a wedge shape which lifts the waistline and gives more fabric across the abdomen. Redraw the waistline from side seam to top of moved section and continue at this height to front seam. Remember that you only add half the amount of extra width required on your pattern piece.

To accommodate a large seat

1 Open the centre back seam at the seat line and add the required extra depth as you would for a long back.

58 Extra room at back of trousers

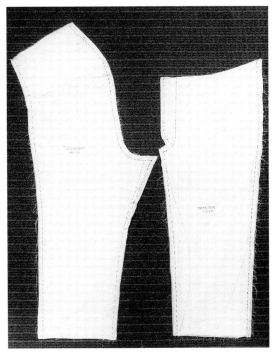

59 Alterations to pattern for Fig. 58

2 In addition, add approximately 1.25 cms ($\frac{1}{2}$ in.) extra at the crotch or fork and down the side seam, narrowing off at knee level. The amount added will vary with each individual (see instructions for people of small stature).
3 For people with a very curved seat, it is wise to put in a front fastening.
Fig. 58 shows comfortable trousers for driving. Fig. 59 gives the pattern. Width has been added at the back fork and inside seam and removed from the outside seam, the trousers fitting snugly round the waist.

To widen the waistline

1 Add one quarter of the extra amount needed to the outside seam at the waist on both patterns.
2 Draw a new side seam from the seat line up to the new waist point.
3 To elasticate the back, draw a line straight up from the seat line to the waistline on the back pattern only.

4 To elasticate the whole waist and eliminate fastenings, draw a straight line up from the seat line to the waistline on both pattern pieces. The waistline must equal the widest part if no fastenings are to be used.

Adapting a trouser pattern for a person of small stature (Fig. 60)

1 Leg length alterations need to be made above and below the knee to keep the proportions correct.
2 Check the pattern measurements from crotch to knee and from knee to hemline

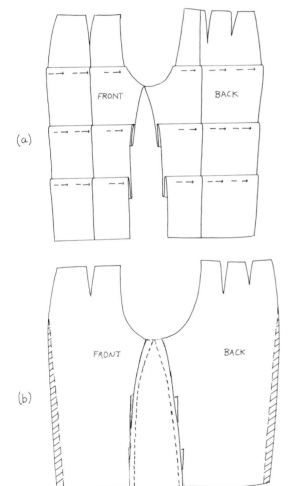

(a)

(b)

60 Trousers for person of small stature

against your own and shorten accordingly. It may be necessary to lower the lengthen/shorten line on the pattern if a large amount is to be folded out.
3 Redraw the side seams to give a good line.
4 Now check the crotch depth measurements, adjust the pattern at seat level, and redraw the seam lines.
5 Measure the new crotch seam length on the pattern and re-check against your own measurements. Now your length will probably be longer than the pattern, and so extra length needs to be added at the fork of the crotch (Fig. 60b). For example: your overall crotch seam length measures 84 cm (33 in.), while the pattern is 76 cm (30 in.); your front waist to crotch seam measures 38 cm (15 in.), while the pattern is 35.5 cm (14 in.). Therefore the front fork needs to be extended by 2.5 cm (1 in.) and the back fork needs to be extended by 5 cm (2 in.).
6 On the inside seam of front and back patterns measure out from the knee half the amount of the extension at the fork. For example: back fork extension 5 cm (2 in.), knee-line extension 2.5 cm (1 in.). Front fork extension 2.5 cm (1 in.), knee-line extension 1.25 cm ($\frac{1}{2}$ in.). Draw a new line from the crotch or fork extension down to the knee and continue it on to the hemline.
7 You now need to remove from the outside leg the same amount that has been added to the inside leg. Measure in the correct amount at the knee. Draw new curve from the crotch line to the knee and continue at the same distance down to the hem.

This is your basic trouser pattern. Make up a trial garment adding extra to the seam allowance but stitching along the pattern or stitch line. Any further alterations can be marked on the garment and recorded on the pattern.

Adapting a trouser pattern for a person who is always seated
(Fig. 61)

1 Make any necessary alterations to the leg length and crotch depth, and widen or narrow the leg if required.
2 Place the front and back patterns together so that the stitching lines of the side seams touch at seat level and the grain lines on the legs are parallel to each other. Pin the pattern pieces together where they overlap.
3 Now draw a line across both pattern pieces half way between the waist and the seat line.
4 On the front pattern, make folds along this line and the seat line at the centre front, so that the crotch seam matches your correct measurement. Shape the folds away to nothing at the side seams.
5 Draw a new centre front seam line.
6 On the back pattern, cut along these lines from the centre back seam to the stitching

line at the side. This will open up two wedge shapes on the centre back seam. Place paper behind the openings and secure.
7 Draw a new back seam line.
8 Measure this line and check it against your back crotch seam measurement. If it is not long enough add extra at the back waist. The fly front will be shortened, but the zip can be extended to the crotch seam if desired.

Cut out a trial pair of trousers, stitch and turn over the seam allowance at waist so tape or string may be slotted through to help fitting. Any excess at the waist can be pinned out, or a note made should extra fabric be needed. Side pockets are often not useable for someone in a wheechair. Patch pockets, where they can be reached easily, are much better. If you do use side pockets remember that they will need altering as well as the pattern.

Altering a Skirt Pattern

Your length measurements have been taken to the floor or foot-rest, and so a further measurement must be taken to determine the height of the hem above the floor or foot-rest. Subtract this last measurement from each of the original measurements to get the correct skirt length at the centre back, centre front and both sides.

Lengthening or shortening a skirt for a symmetrical figure

This is usually done at the hemline, but it can be done at the lengthen/shorten line on the pattern.

Correcting the skirt waistline

Many people with sway backs need fabric taken out of the centre back at the waistline, while others who lean forward will need the front shortened.

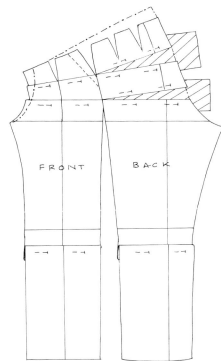

FRONT   BACK

61 Alterations for sit-down trousers

87

1 Check your side waist to hem measurement against the pattern and alter the length if necessary.

2 Measure from the hemline to the centre front waist, and from the hemline to the centre back waist, and re-shape the waistline to match your measurements.

For those who lean forward considerably:

1 Place the front and back pattern pieces side seam to side seam, and pin the stitching lines together.

2 Cut along the hip-line on the back pattern from the centre back to the side seam. (This will open up the back pattern and lengthen the back seam similar to the trousers in Fig. 61.)

3 Fold out the front pattern at the centre front until the correct waist to hem measurement is obtained. The resulting wedge folds away to nothing at the side seam.

Adding or removing width to or from the skirt

Check your waist and hip measurements against the pattern envelope or your personal measurement chart. A multi-sized pattern is very useful if your measurements are not standard. Up to 5 cm (2 in.) can be added or removed from a skirt at the side seams. Divide any difference in size between you and the pattern by four and add or take away that amount from each side seam.

Adapting a skirt pattern for a person of short stature

A person of small stature will tend to curve out more quickly from the waist to the hips and may need the back waist dipped slightly. The hip-line on a bought pattern is 18–23 cm (7–9 in.) below the waistline (18 cm [7 in.] on the Miss Petite and Half Size and 23 cm [9 in.] on the Womens and Misses).

1 Check the distance from the widest part of the hips to your waist and adjust the pattern to your measurements by folding

out the required amount halfway between the waist and the hip-line.

2 Make any necessary alterations at the waistline and re-draw the side seam.

3 Where the fold in the pattern creates a step out in the side seam, draw the new seam line half-way through the step.

Elastic-waisted skirts can be useful. You can either leave the darts unstitched, keep the zipped opening, and elasticate the waistband, or cut the pattern straight up from the hips on both front and back patterns, elasticate the waistline and eliminate all fastenings.

Adapting a skirt pattern for an asymmetrical figure/or scoliosis (Figs. 62a and 62b)

The aim is to get the skirt to hang straight from the hip and fit snugly at the waist.

1 Trace a copy of both front and back patterns and stick the two fronts together and the two backs together along the centre line to form a complete pattern. (Lengthen or shorten to give a correct front waist to hemline measurement.)

2 Draw a line across the pattern pieces at the hip and a second line 8 cm (3 in.) above the hip if you have a short figure, or 10 cm (4 in.) above the hip if you are taller.

3 On your longer side, cut along these lines from the side seam to the centre on both front and back pattern pieces.

4 Check the difference between the pattern measurement and your measurement from waist to hem on your shorter side.

5 At the side seam, fold away the extra amount along these two lines. The fold should fade away to nothing at the centre front and centre back. This will open out the opposite side.

6 Secure paper behind the openings and re-shape the side seams.

7 Check the longer side measurement

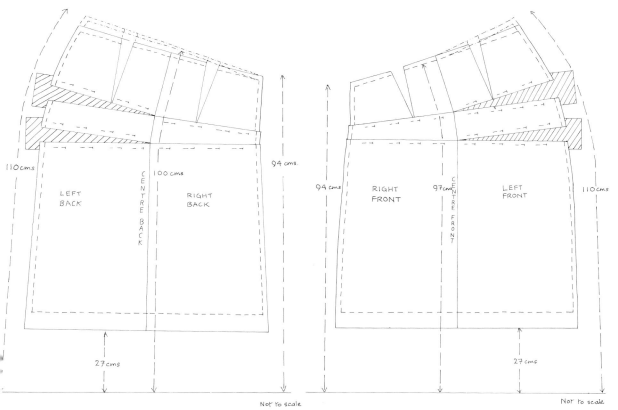

110cms   100 cms   94 cms.

LEFT
BACK

C
E
N
T
R
E

B
A
C
K

RIGHT
BACK

27cms

Not to scale

94 cms   97cms   110cms

RIGHT
FRONT

C
E
N
T
R
E

F
R
O
N
T

LEFT
FRONT

27cms

Not to scale

62 *above* Skirt pattern for scoliosis   63 *below* Pleated skirt pattern for scoliosis

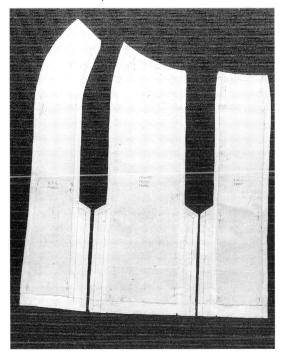

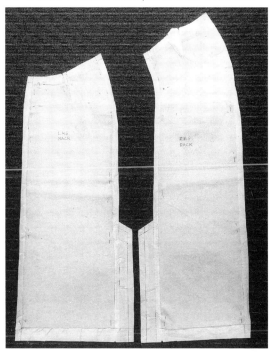

against your own. If it is not long enough add extra at the waistline.

8 Check the centre back to hem measurement and add any extra that may be needed at the waist.

9 Re-shape waistline.

10 Make a toile and check that the fabric hangs straight and that the hemline is straight. Tie a string around the waist to check the waistline shape. Mark any alterations first on the 'toile' and then transfer back onto the paper pattern.

If the distance from the floor to the hemline is 27 cm (10½ in.) then the skirt lengths will be as follows:

Centre front to hem = 70 cm (27½ in.) – adjusted.

Right side to hem = 66 cm (26 in.) – folded out.

Left side to hem = 84 cm (33 in.) – opened out and extra added at waist.

Centre back to hem – 74 cm (29 in.) – extra added.

Figs 63a and 63b Show patterns for a pleated skirt for a scoliosis.

Altering Jacket, Shirt, Blouse or Bodice Patterns

Shoulders (Fig. 64)

To *narrow* the shoulder seam on the front and back bodice pattern:

1 Make a diagonal cut to the shoulder seam one-third of the way in from the armhole and finish the cut half-way down the armhole seam, stopping at the stitching line.

2 Overlap the pieces until the shoulder is the correct length.

3 Re-draw the shoulder line from shoulder point to neck point.

To *widen*, open the pieces out until the correct length is obtained and re-draw the shoulder line as above.

To shorten the front bodice for those who lean forward (Fig. 65a)

1 For shirts, blouses, dresses or jackets, fold out the amount necessary to give the correct centre front measurement and ease the fold away to nothing at the side

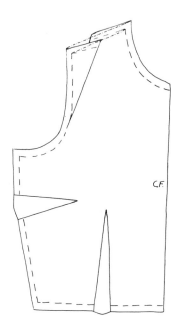

64 Altering shoulder length

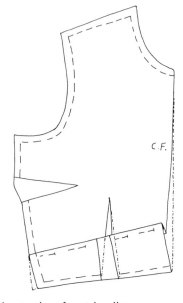

65a Shortening front bodice

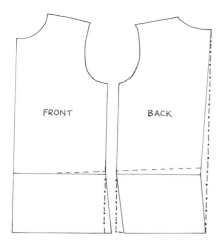

65b Shortening back bodice

seams. Occasionally the fold needs to follow through the side seam a little way and finish in the back bodice, depending on the shape of the individual. This will become apparent when fitting the trial garment.

2 Draw a new centre front line from the neck to the waist or hemline.

3 The fold will have tilted the side seam, so re-draw the seam in its original position, adding extra to the front bodice and removing the same amount from the back bodice.

4 For garments with a waist seam, tie a string around the waist when the toile is fitted and mark where the waistline needs to be.

To shorten the back bodice for a sway back (Fig. 65b)

Alter the back bodice in a similar way to the front bodice.

Surplus fabric in a jacket back usually needs to be removed at the waistline. You may prefer to do this when fitting the toile. (Fig. 66.)

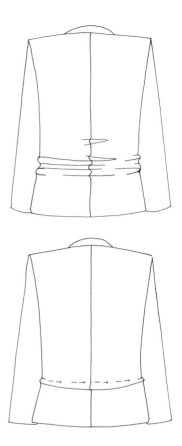

66 Removing excess at waist

To lengthen the centre back for those who lean forward (Fig. 67)

Patterns with a back seam or a back yoke are most easily altered. For a style with a centre back seam:

1 Cut the pattern across from the centre back to a point between one-third and half way down the armhole. Stop at the stitching line.

2 Open the centre back until the correct measurement is obtained.

3 Place extra paper behind the opening and secure.

4 Re-draw the back seam. If you prefer to have the back seam straight continue the centre back line up to neck level and remove excess created at neckline in a dart.

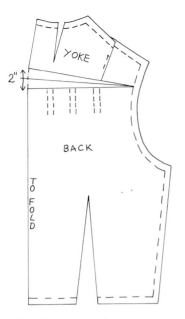

67 Lengthening the back

For patterns with a yoke:

1 Cut off or fold back the seam allowances at the bottom of the yoke and the top of the back bodice.
2 Pleat or tuck the bodice pattern until it fits the yoke.
3 Place the two together, then open the centre back seam to the required amount and secure extra paper behind the opening.
4 Draw a line half way between the yoke and the bodice from the centre back to the armhole stitching line and cut along it.

This will extend both the yoke and the back.

5 The back bodice will need one or two vertical cuts to enable the pattern to open out to full width when the pleats are released.
6 Put more paper behind and draw a new line following the edges of the cut paper. Add seam allowances.

Additional alterations at the trial garment stage and later

1 Try the garment on, pin at the centre front or centre back, and tie a string around the natural waist. This will enable you to mark the correct waistline.
2 If you have uneven shoulders you may be happy with a shoulder pad on one side, or a thick pad on one side and a thinner pad in the other to even out the shoulders. If no pads are used, pin the shoulders seams to fit correctly.
3 You may find that the neckline is too big, too small or uneven. If the back neck has too much fabric pin out the excess fabric to give a good fit, either at the centre back seam or by making two neck darts (see Fig. 68). Now mark where the neckline should be and cut away or let in extra fabric.
4 Many people in wheelchairs find that a fold appears in a garment across the shoulder blades after they have worn it for

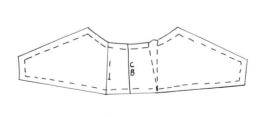

68 Removing excess at back neck

a short time. A yoked style will enable you to dispose of the excess fabric easily when it becomes apparent.

Alterations for a kyphosis, or hump back (Fig. 69)

1 When the toile is completed cut along the centre back between the waist and the neck, and across the back to each armhole at the point where the back is at its widest. Do not cut through the seam allowances.
2 When worn the garment will open out at the centre and across the back, making it wider and longer.
3 Place extra fabric inside the toile and pin it into position.

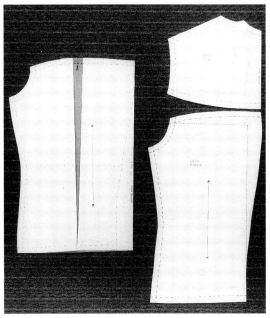

70 Pattern adaptation for kyphosis

4 Re-draw centre back line and line across back.

The best style to design is one with a yoke. Fig. 70 (right) shows the shape of the remodelled yoke and bodice back. To add a pleat or tuck, draw a vertical line down, parallel to the grain line, from half way along the top of the pattern. Cut down this line to open up a wedge 2.5 cm (1 in.) for a tuck, or a little more if you wish to gather the back (Fig. 70, [left]).

Alterations for people of small stature

To alter a one-piece garment (Fig. 71a)

1 If the sleeve is too tight around the top arm cut the sleeve along the lengthwise grain from the shoulder point to the wrist, leaving the seam allowances intact.
2 At the underarm corner, open out the pattern to the required width and fold away excess pattern across the centre. Taper the fold away to the corner to make the pattern lie flat.

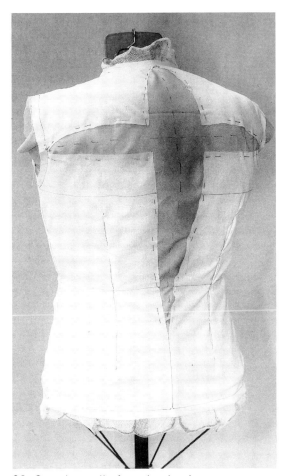

69 Opening toile for a kyphosis

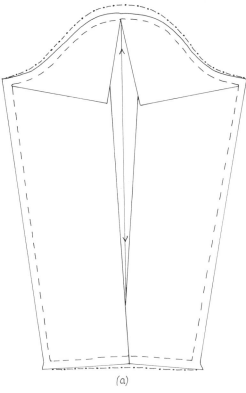

(a)

adding width to top arm

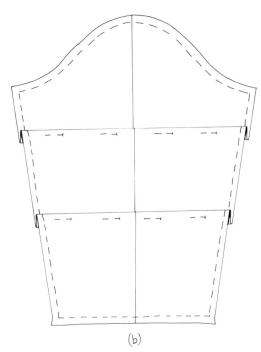

(b)

shortening sleeve

71a Sleeve for person of small stature

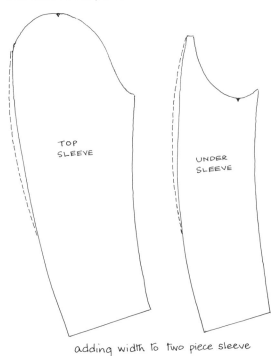

TOP
SLEEVE

UNDER
SLEEVE

adding width to two piece sleeve

71b Two-piece sleeve

3 Re-draw the sleeve head to keep the armhole the same size.
4 Re-draw the hemline and the grain line down the centre of the opening.
5 Now reduce the length above and below the elbow.

To alter a two-piece sleeve (Fig. 71b)
Reduce the length above and below the elbow on each pattern piece. Half any extra width needed should be added to the back seam on each piece.

To shorten or lengthen a jacket or bodice (Fig. 72a)
This means adjusting the pattern to give the correct neck to waist measurement. The bodice pattern will give one shorten/ lengthen line but another may be added.
A waisted dress may be shortened at the waistline to accommodate a sway back or, alternatively, the waistline may be elasticated to create a blouson effect.

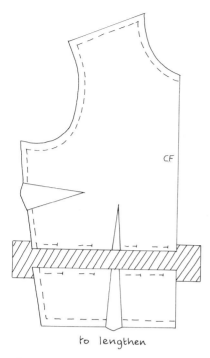

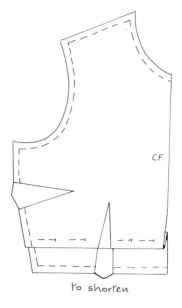

to shorten

to lengthen

72a Lengthening and shortening bodice

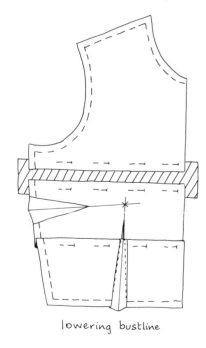

lowering bustline

72b Altering bust position

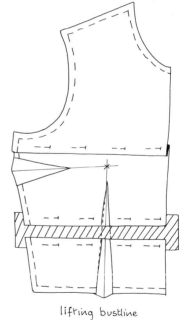

lifting bustline

To alter position of bust line on front bodice (Fig. 72b)

1 Cut across the pattern above the dart.
2 Let in or remove the amount necessary to give correct bust position.
3 Let in or take out the same amount below dart.

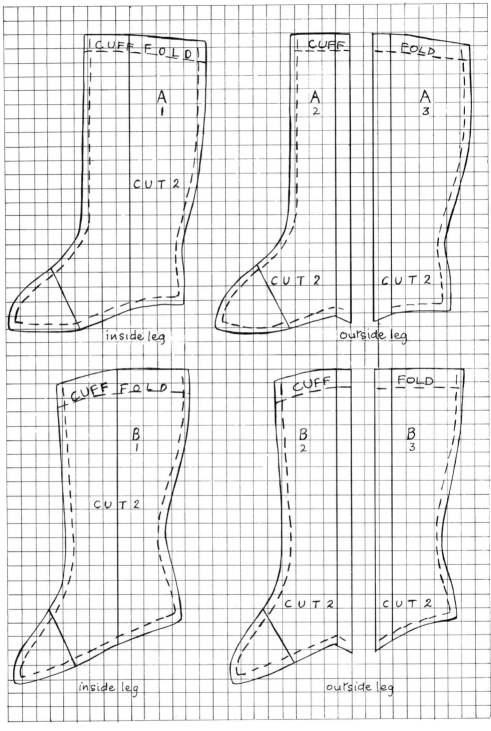

1 square = 2.5 cms. (1 in)

73a Spat pattern

One-off Patterns

Spats (Figs. 73a and 73b)

Before measuring the leg check whether the person in the wheelchair prefers to sit with his or her legs straight down from the knee or at an angle. Pattern A is for a straight leg, pattern B for those who sit with their feet slightly forward.

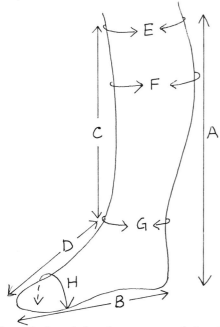

A *Length from below knee to top of shoe heel.*
B *Length from centre back heel to centre front toe.*
C *Length from below knee to ankle joint.*
D *Length from ankle joint to toe.*
E *Round leg below knee.*
F *Round calf (widest part).*
G *Round ankle.*
H *Over foot at widest part from shoe sole to shoe sole.*

73b Measurement chart

(The pattern allows 2.5 cm [1 in.] ease for fur fabric.)

1 Draw a full-sized pattern following the grid for style A or B.
2 Now measure the leg, taking measurements A through to H, and check the differences between you and the pattern.

3 To reduce width down the whole of the leg, fold out half the necessary amount down the centre of the outside leg and take a quarter of the amount away from the centre seam of each inside leg.
4 To widen the whole leg, cut down the centre of the outside leg pattern and space the two pieces apart by half the required amount.
5 Up to 5 cm (2 in.) can be added or removed at any point by adding or subtracting half the amount down the back seam.
6 Length can be added or removed by letting in or folding out the required amount at calf level. To lengthen or shorten between the ankle joint and the toe, cut along the line indicated and move the piece away until the correct measurement is reached, or fold on this line. Re-draw foot outline to give good shape.
8 Extend the pattern A2 by 2.5 cm (1 in.) to make a facing. Follow the shaping for the bottom as shown on the grid, so that when the facing is turned back it follows the line of the foot.
9 Extend pattern A3 by 2.5 cm (1 in.) to make an underlap.
10 Sew centre front and back seams, open out and stitch seam allowances flat.
11 Fold the facing of pattern A2 under and stitch flat.
12 Neaten the edge of pattern A3, underlap.
13 Neaten the bottom edge, turn under and stitch in position.
14 If fur fabric is used neaten, turn to the right side and stitch cuff down. For other fabric, neaten, fold seam allowance to wrong side and stitch.

Pop-on sweatshirt fronts (Fig. 74a)

1 Trace around the front pattern or bodice, excluding seam allowances.
2 Draw on to the traced bodice the shape of the front panel you would like and cut out. Add seam allowances.

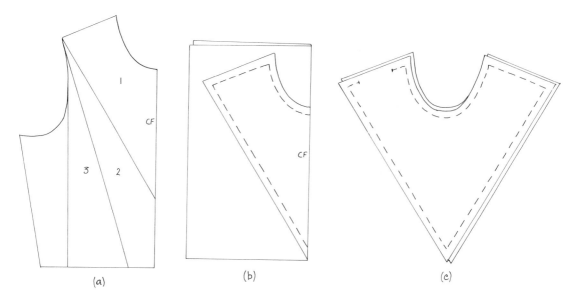

74a Pop-on fronts

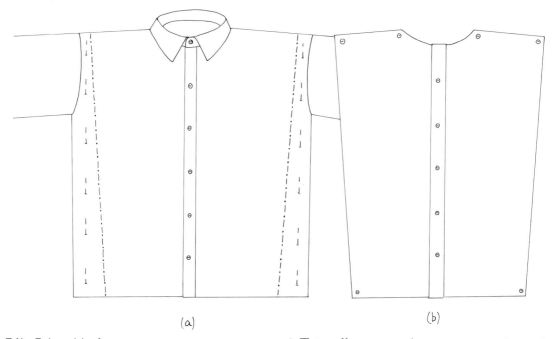

74b False shirt fronts

3 Place the centre of this pattern on to a fold of the chosen fabric and cut out.

4 Cut again in a waterproof fabric.

5 With right sides together, stitch around the edges, leaving a small opening on one shoulder.

6 Trim all seams and corners, turn through to the right side and hand sew to close the opening.

7 Tack around the edges, top stitch, and then remove the tacking.

8 Attach poppers or press-studs to the waterproof side of the front and to the right side of the garment in the same positions. It is wise to put a small piece of iron-on Vilene behind the popper on the garment to give extra strength.

If preferred, buttons can be put on the sweatshirt, and buttonholes on the false front.

False fronts for shirts (Fig. 74b)

If the shirt has a yoke it is easier to make a pattern from the finished garment:

1 Lay the shirt out flat, buttoned to the top, on to a sheet of paper.
2 Draw along the shoulder lines, side seams, and shirt bottom, and mark vertically the centre front.
3 Mark from the neck your personal shoulder measurement.
4 Mark one half of the neckline by pin-pricking through to the paper every 1 cm ($\frac{1}{2}$ in.), finishing at the centre front.
5 Remove the shirt.
6 Draw a line down the centre front.
7 Draw a curve for the neckline, following the pin pricks.
8 Draw a line from the chosen shoulder point to the hem, sloping in slightly towards the centre.

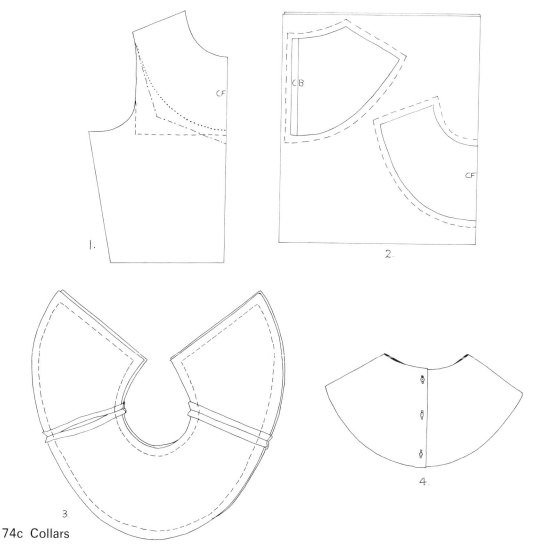

74c Collars

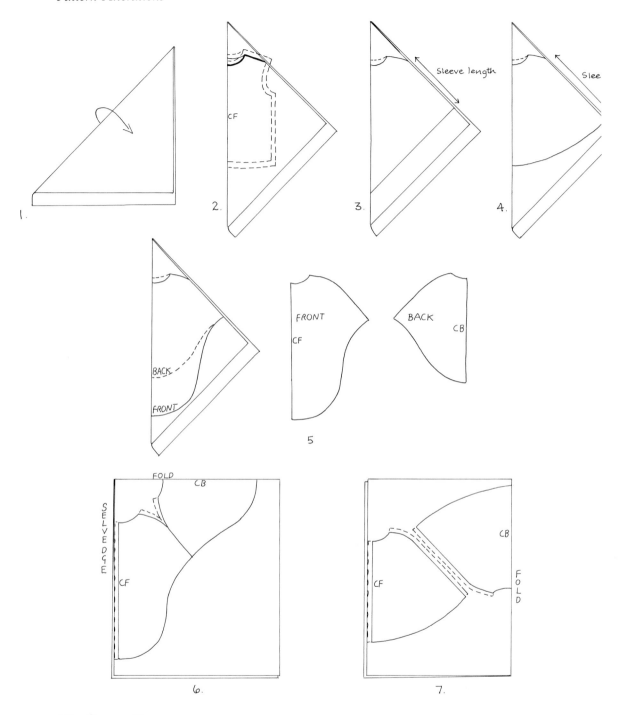

75a Cape pattern

9 Cut out as for sweatshirt fronts.

10 A strip of fabric stitched down the centre front, with buttons added, will match the appearance of the original shirt.

11 Stitch and complete as for sweatshirts.

False collars (Fig. 74c)

1 Trace around the neck and shoulder seams of the front and back bodice patterns. Do not include the seam allowances.

2 Draw the required collar shape on both patterns (Diagram 1).

3 Cut out the pattern piece and add 1 cm ($\frac{1}{2}$ in.) to the centre back for the overlap.

4 Fold in half the fabric to be used.

5 Place the centre of the front collar on the fold and the back collar elsewhere on the fabric. Add seam allowances to all edges except to the fold (Diagram 2).

6 Cut out, and repeat in a waterproof fabric for the lining.

7 Join both shoulder seams on the fabric but only one seam on the waterproof lining. Join the other lining seam for a short distance at each end. Fold back all remaining seam allowances.

8 With right sides together, machine around the neckline, down each centre back and around the outside of the collar (Diagram 3).

9 Trim, turn through the gap in one seam, and press gently on the top side.

10 Work buttonholes 1 cm ($\frac{1}{2}$ in.) in from the edge on the left back, and sew buttons 1 cm ($\frac{1}{2}$ in.) from the edge on the right back (Diagram 4).

Quick cape pattern (Fig. 75a)

1 Take a large sheet of paper approximately 1 m (39 in.) square and fold it at 45° to make a right-angled triangle (Diagram 1).

2 Turn the paper so that the diagonal is upright.

3 Using the front bodice pattern of a blouse or dress with a round neck and set-in sleeves, place the centre front of the bodice on the diagonal fold line, and position it so that the stitching line at the outer end of the shoulder touches the edge of the paper (Diagram 2).

4 Using a tracing wheel, mark along the stitching lines of the neck and shoulder (Diagram 2).

5 Remove the front pattern, and replace with the back pattern, matching the shoulder seams and the centre with the fold.

6 Trace the back neckline and remove the back pattern.

7 Follow the shoulder line down the side of the paper to the required sleeve length and mark.

8 You now have the choice of a number of styles:

A poncho style. From the sleeve mark, draw a line, parallel to the bottom edge, across to the centre fold (diagram 3).

A rounded cape (Diagram 4).

A curved cape. The curve may be a shorter, i.e. chair-length, at the back, and longer at the front. Mark the pattern for the back with a tracing wheel.

9 Cut the front pattern from the top fold, and the back pattern from the under fold (Diagram 5). There are no seam allowances at this stage.

10 Depending upon the width of the fabric and the size of the pattern, you may be able to plan a pattern layout for a one-piece cape (Diagram 6), or a three-piece cape (Diagram 7).

11 Add seam allowances at the neck, shoulder and centre front of the one-piece, or at the neck, sides and centre front of the three-piece cape.

12 Cut out and stitch the shoulder dart (Diagram 6), or the side seams (Diagram 7).

13 Stitch the front seam, leaving an opening for a zip or decorative fastening.

14 Insert the zip, then bind the neckline and hemline with braid. The cape can be

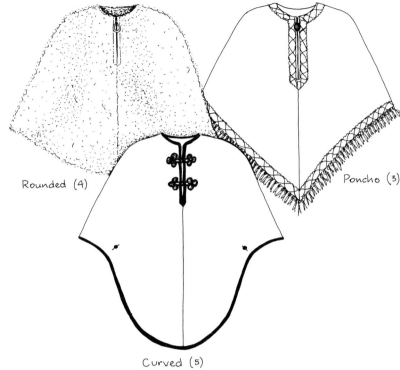

Rounded (4)

Poncho (3)

Curved (5)

75b Cape styles

lined if desired and can have a button
fastening to give a 'sleeve' opening.
Fig. 75b shows various cape styles.

Open-crotch knicker patterns
(Fig. 76a and 76b)

Pattern A is for a pantie style, pattern B is for
a brief, and pattern C is for a long-legged
knicker with a catheter pocket. A knitted
fabric is essential for these patterns.

1 For patterns A and B, cut two backs and
one front on the fold. For pattern C, cut
two.

2 For patterns A, B and C, turn under the
seam allowance on the centre seam of
each back and neaten with a stretch or
zig-zag stitch.

For patterns A and B:

3 Overlap the two backs, matching at the
centre back notches at top and bottom.
Pin in position.

4 Place the pinned backs on a table or flat

surface, right side up, and place the front
on top, right side down, matching the
waist and side seams.

5 Fold the back overlapped gusset up to
meet the front crotch seam and pin the
seam, right sides together. Stitch, trim
and then neaten with a stretch or zig-zag
stitch to give a flat seam.

6 Stitch the side seams and neaten.

7 Turn under the seam allowance at the
waistband and legs and neaten with a
stretch or zig-zag stitch. At the same time
picot-edged elastic may be added to give a
functional and decorative finish.

For pattern C proceed as follows after No. 2:

8 Stitch the centre front seams together
and neaten with a stretch or zig-zag stitch.

9 Cut a pocket large enough to accommodate the catheter bag.

10 Turn under the seam allowance at the
pocket top and neaten with a decorative
elastic.

11 Turn under the other seam allowances

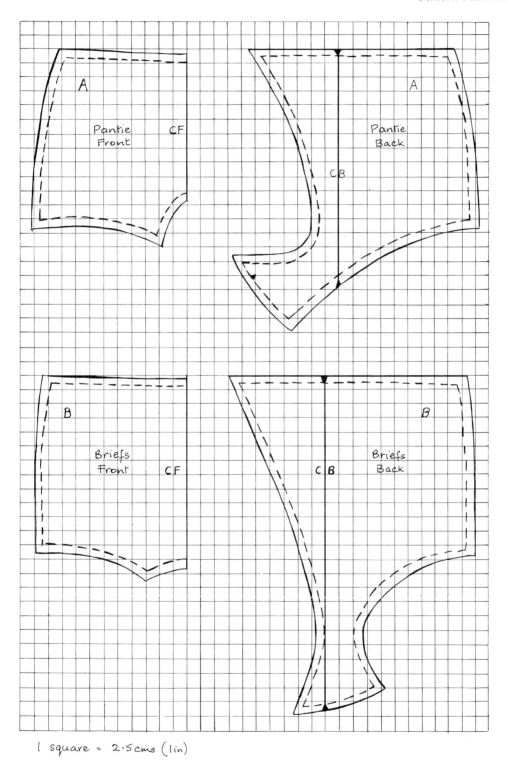

1 square = 2.5 cms (1 in)

76a Open-crotch brief and pantie pattern

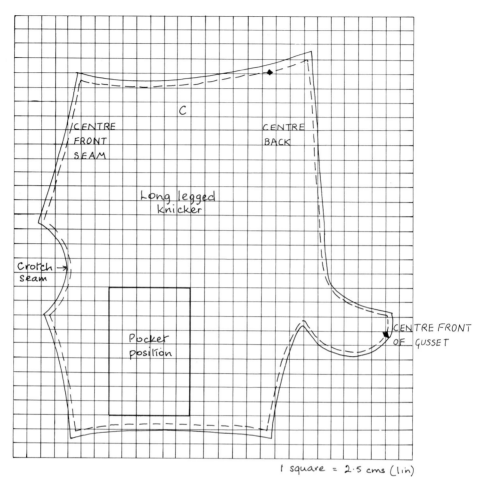

C

CENTRE
FRONT
SEAM

CENTRE
BACK

Long legged
knicker

Crotch →
seam

CENTRE FRONT
OF GUSSET

Pocket
position

1 square = 2·5 cms (1 in)

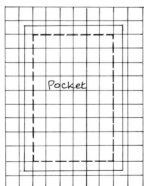

Pocket

76b Long-legged knicker pattern

and sew to the front of one leg, leaving a gap in the stitching at the bottom to accommodate the tube which empties the catheter bag.

12 Overlap the two neatened backs, matching the centre back and centre front notches. Pin in position.

13 Place the garment flat on a table with the centre front seam directly over the centre back.

14 Fold the gusset over from the back and match the centre front notch of the gusset with the centre front seam.

15 Pin the overlapped gussets to the crotch seam and pin down each leg.

16 Stitch, trim and neaten to make a flat seam.

17 Complete the waistband and legs as for patterns A and B.

Heel-less socks for men or women

Materials: Double knitting yarn (5 oz for a short length, 7 oz for a regular length). Set of four 3 mm (No. 11) needles with points at both ends.

Measurements: For short or regular length.

Tension: $6\frac{3}{4}$ sts and nine rows to one square inch on 3 mm (No. 11) needles, measured over stocking stitch.

Cast on 64 sts on No. 3 needles, join for round.

Knit in K2, P2 rib for 5 cm (2 in.).

Proceed in patterns as follows:

1st to 3rd round: *K2, P2, repeat from * to end of round.

4th to 6th round: P1, *K2, P2, repeat from * to last 3 sts, K2 P1.

7th to 9th round: *P2, K2, repeat from * to end of round.

10th to 12th round: K1, *P2, K2, repeat from * to last 3 sts, P2, K1.

These 12 rounds form the spiral pattern.

For short socks:

Continue in pattern until work measures 29 cm ($11\frac{1}{2}$ in.) (sock size 9), 30.5 cm (12 in.) (sock size 10), 32 cm ($12\frac{1}{2}$ in.) (sock size 11), 33 cm (13 in.) (sock size 12).

For regular sock:

Continue in pattern till work measures 47 cm ($18\frac{1}{2}$ in.) (sock size 9), 48 cm (19 in.) (sock size 10), 49.5 cm ($19\frac{1}{2}$ in.) (sock size 11), 51 cm (20 in.) (sock size 12).

Divide sts: 16 on first needle, 32 on second needle, 16 on third needle.

1st round: On first needle K to last 3 sts, K2 tog, K1. On 2nd needle K1, K2 tog. t.b.1., knit to last 3 sts, K2 tog K1. On 3rd needle K1, K2 tog. t.b.1., K to end.

2nd round: Knit.

Repeat these rounds until 12 sts remain. Graft together 2 sets of 6 sts to finish toe. The pattern repeats on four stitches and can have a number of stitches divisible by four either added or taken away to change the width of the socks. The use of larger needles to start with, coming down to smaller ones allows room for chubby calves. The use of 4-ply wool and size $2\frac{3}{4}$ mm (No. 12) needles would again change the width for children. Knit a small piece in stocking stitch to measure your tension, measure the calf or top of leg and multiply the measurement by the number of stitches per 2.5 cm (1 in.), bring this down to the nearest number divisible by four. For example, top leg measures 33 cm (13 in.). My tension is 7 stitches × 9 rows to 2.5 cm (1 in.). Number of stitches required = 88.

9 ALTERING READY-MADE GARMENTS

Altering a ready-made garment can be a time-consuming business, involving careful unpicking and re-stitching. But for disabled people it may make all the difference in the world. What was a sloppy, oversized and ill-fitting garment can become bright and smart and well-fitting so that it looks as though it belongs to the wearer. Knowing that your clothes fit you and suit you has a great psychological impact.

Altering Foundation Garments and Underwear

A front-fastening bra
(see Fig. 32 on p. 52)

1 Remove the hook-and-eye section from the front of the bra, and in its place insert a fine zip 10–15 cm (4–6 in.) longer than the bra opening. The length depends on the room needed to put it on easily. Use a nylon zip that has no teeth showing on the back when it is fastened.
2 Sew the zip in with two rows of stitching to hold the tape flat.
3 Add a loop of ribbon at the bottom of the zip, and a ribbon loop through the zipper slide.
4 A bra-slip should have the back opening stitched up and replaced with a new zipped opening in the front.

Girdles (see Fig. 32 on p. 52)

A hooked, side-fastening girdle can be treated in a similar way to a bra.
1 Remove the hooks, and replace with a nylon zip slightly longer than the garment to allow it to open wider and give easier access.
2 Stitch two long loops to the sides of the girdle at the top. This should enable you to get it nearer to your feet.

A step-in girdle is very difficult to put on if you have lost your grip. These can be altered by inserting two zips.
1 If the girdle has a centre front panel replace the seams with zips, one starting at the top, the other at the bottom.
2 If not, cut the girdle from the top about 6 cm ($2\frac{3}{8}$ in.) away from the centre front on the right side and extend the cut to within 1 cm ($\frac{1}{2}$ in.) of the bottom. Make a second cut on the left side, but start 6 cm ($2\frac{3}{8}$ in.) away from the centre at the bottom, and extend to within 1 cm ($\frac{1}{2}$ in.) of the top.
3 Overlock or zig-zag the edges, and insert the zips. The right side will have the zip slide at the top when fastened, while on the left side the slide will be at the bottom.

When the zips are opened there will be much more room to put the girdle on. Loops may also be stitched to the side of the girdle, and to the zipper slides.

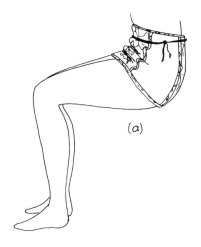

(a)   (b)

77 Shaping a girdle

Shaping a girdle (Fig. 77)

If you are sitting all day the girdle may be more comfortable if it is shaped at the front.
1 Tie a piece of string around your waist and mark the position of the string with tailors' chalk or a soft pencil.
2 Unpick the elastic binding as far as necessary, cut the girdle to within a seam allowance of the markings, and replace the binding using a stretch machine stitch.
3 To shape the lower front, mark from the back, around the curve of the thigh and across the top of the legs.
4 Cut and finish as for the waistline. Soft elastic, available at haberdashery shops, can be used as a binding, and will give extra stretch at the edges.

Men's underwear
(see Fig. 29 on p. 50)

Y-fronts can be difficult to manipulate. Trunks are often better as the front overlap goes right down to the crotch seam. The row of stitching 5 cm ($2\frac{1}{2}$ in.) above the crotch seam can be removed and repeated much nearer to the crotch, extending the opening considerably.

Women's briefs to wear with full-length calipers (Fig. 78)

1 Unpick the front seam of the gusset as in Fig 78a.
2 Cut a bias strip of fabric in the same fibre as the briefs, 2.5 cm (1 in.) wide × length of seam, plus 5 cm (2 in.).
3 With right sides together, machine the strip on to the front of the briefs taking a 5 mm ($\frac{1}{4}$ in.) seam.
4 Trim the edges of the strip to the shape of the briefs, leaving 0.5 cm ($\frac{1}{4}$ in.) seam allowance at each side (Fig. 78b).
5 Turn the strip to the wrong side of the garment, turn in the allowances at either end and along the curved edge.
6 Tack and machine with a stretch stitch (Fig. 78c).
7 For the gusset edge, cut a bias strip the same length as previously but 4 cm ($1\frac{1}{2}$ in.) wide. Fold in half lengthways and press.
8 With right sides together, machine one side of the strip to the gusset, 0.5 cm ($\frac{1}{4}$ in.) from the edge (Fig. 78d).
9 Turn the strip to the right side, press the seam and fold.
10 Trim the ends to fit the shape of the front brief, leaving a 0.5 cm ($\frac{1}{4}$ in.) seam allowance (Fig. 78e).
11 Turn in the 0.5 cm ($\frac{1}{4}$ in.) seam allowance on the remaining length of the strip, then

107

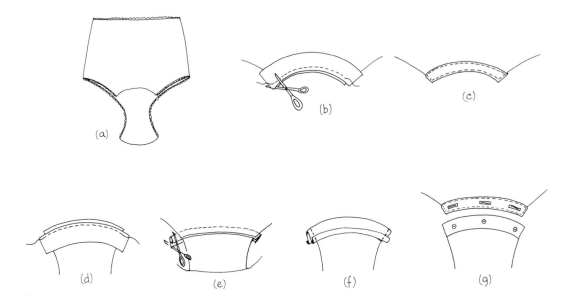

78 Briefs alteration for full-length calipers

fold back the strip right sides together and machine each end (Fig. 78f).

12 Turn back to the right side and machine or hem stitch the final curve.

13 Make three buttonholes in the band on the front brief and the gusset band (Fig. 78g).

Press-studs or Velcro spot-ons could be used if preferred.

Changing Fastenings and their Positions

Replacing buttons with Velcro spot-ons (see Fig. 33 on p. 53)

Remove the buttons and stitch on to the buttonhole band, in the centre of vertical bottonholes, or at the centre front end of horizontal buttonholes. The soft half on the spot-on is sewn beneath each button by hand. The hooked half is sewn where the button was originally, and can be machined or hand sewn.

Managing cuffs without undoing the fastening (see Fig. 33 on p. 53)

Method 1:
Join the two buttons together with shirring elastic to form a stretching cufflink. Take a needle twice through each button to give four threads across, approximately 2.5 cm (1 in.) long. Buttonhole or blanket stitch over the threads. Use as for cufflinks. The stretch will allow the hand to pass through without unfastening the button.

Method 2:
Cuff buttons can also be sewn on with shirring elastic. Place a matchstick between the button and the cuff as you sew. This will produce a shank when the match is removed. Wind the elastic round the shank and fasten off.

Adding a front placket to a back-zipped dress (Fig. 79)

(This will give more room for dressing.)
1 Remove the collar, facing or binding around the neck.

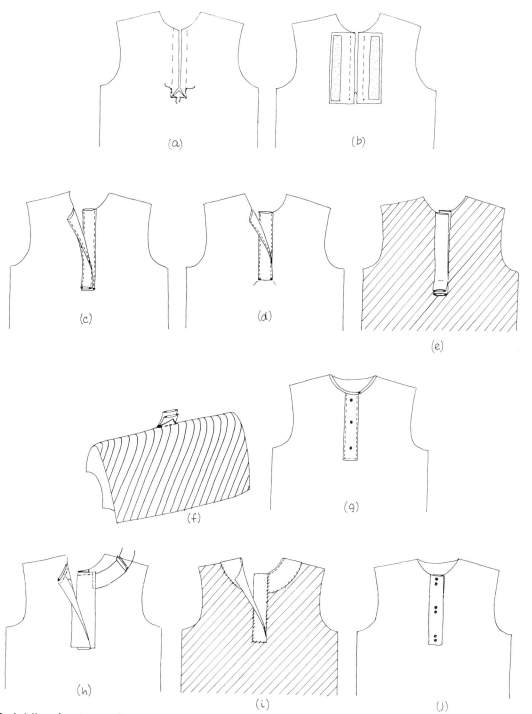

79 Adding front opening

2 Find the centre front of the dress and mark with a thread the required length of the opening.

3 Mark a seam allowance of 1.5 cm ($\frac{5}{8}$ in.) down each side and across the bottom. Machine at the corners to give strength.

4 Cut down the centre front and out to each corner (Fig. 79a).

5 Using a similar fabric to the dress in a matching or contrasting colour, cut two strips 9 cm (3$\frac{1}{2}$ in.) wide × length of opening, plus 2 cm ($\frac{3}{4}$ in.). Fold in half lengthways and press.

6 Iron a length of fine Vilene interlining to half of each strip.

7 Tack and machine one strip to each side of the opening on the right side, fastening off well at the bottom corners (Fig. 79b).

If you wish to bind the neck edge proceed as follows:

8 Press each piece towards the centre at the seam. Fold in half, turn in the seam allowance and stitch (Fig. 79c).

9 Push the bottom of the strips through to the wrong side (Figs. 79d and 79e).

10 Fold the bodice back on a level with the base of the opening, and stitch across the 'V' to catch the two plackets (Fig. 79f).

11 Bind the neckline with a bias strip, and stitch on buttons, poppers or Velcro. Fig 79g shows the finished opening.

If you prefer to face the neckline complete the strips as far as stage 7, then:

12 Trace off the neck and shoulder lines from the front and back bodice and cut facings 7 cm (3$\frac{1}{2}$ in.) deep, with an opening at the centre front.

13 Place the centre front edge of each facing on to the unstitched edge of the strip right side to right side, and stitch down the depth of the facing starting at the neck edge. Stitch shoulder seams of the facings together (Fig. 79h).

14 Fold the strips in half, right sides together, then tack and machine the complete facing to the garment neckline. Trim and snip the seams.

15 Press the facing and seam allowances away from the bodice, and then understitch the facing 25 mm ($\frac{1}{8}$ in.) from the seam line.

16 Turn the plackets through to their right side and complete the outside seam of each placket (Fig. 79i).

17 Push the bottom of the plackets through to the wrong side and stitch across the 'V'.

18 Neaten the raw edges of the facing and catch at the shoulder seams. A bought collar, lacey or plain, could be added if desired (Fig. 79j).

Opening the back seam of a jacket or coat
(see Fig. 36a and 36b on p. 57)

1 Unpick the back seam of the jacket as far as the collar. If the lining has no seam cut it up the centre to the back neck.

2 Unpick a little of the hem to either side of the opening.

3 Cut a strip of fabric 8 cm, (3 in.) wide and the length of the jacket plus 3 cm, (1$\frac{1}{4}$ in.). If you can match the fabric to the jacket, fine; if not, use a contrasting colour and repeat it in a scarf, or use a tone of the same colour.

4 Fold the band in half lengthways, with right sides together, and stitch 1.5 cm, ($\frac{5}{8}$ in.) seams across the top and bottom.

5 Trim the corners, turn through to the right side and press.

6 Place the right side of the coat, with its seam allowance folded back 1.5 cm, ($\frac{5}{8}$ in.) over the raw edges of the band, and machine stitch close to the edge.

7 Turn the hem back up on this side and stitch over the raw edges.

8 Turn in the edge of the lining and catch down along the stitching line of the band.

9 On the left-hand side, fold up the hem allowance with the right sides of fabric together and machine along the old seam line. Trim the corner and turn through.

10 Turn in a seam allowance on the coat and

the lining and hand stitch the lining to the coat about 3 mm, ($\frac{1}{8}$ in.) from the edge. Flat buttons and buttonholes, or Velcro spot-ons can be used to fasten the opening. For a short jacket, a zip could be inserted into the back seam, with or without the added strip. The method of fastening depends on the individual and whether pressure sores are a consideration.

Altering Outerwear for Wheelchair Users

Shortening anorak sleeves
(see Fig. 23 on p. 47)

The alteration will automatically shorten the sleeve by 4 cm ($1\frac{1}{2}$ in.).

1 Cut the sleeve across 5–7$\frac{1}{2}$ cm, (2–3 in.) above the elbow. If it needs shortening more than 4 cm ($1\frac{1}{2}$ in.) cut the extra away from the lower sleeve.
2 Neaten the edge of the lower sleeve either by binding with a bias strip, or it may be possible to turn in 0.5 cm, ($\frac{1}{4}$ in.) seams on the coat and lining and stitch the two together.
3 Re-shape the seam on the upper sleeve to give a good fit, and neaten to match the lower sleeve.
4 Slot the lower sleeve inside the upper sleeve to give a 3 cm, ($1\frac{1}{4}$ in.) overlap.
5 Attach poppers.

Shortening the back of a coat

1 Put the coat on and mark where it touches the chair at the back.
2 A straight style may need a vent. In this case, unpick the side seams up 10 cm, (4 in.) above the chair-length marks.
3 Cut off the back of the coat a hem allowance below the chair-length marks. (Be guided by the depth of the hem already on the coat.)
4 If no vent is needed machine the side

seams to the required length for the back, leaving the hem free. Fasten off securely.
5 Turn up the hem along the back of the coat and catch stitch. Catch the edges of the hems to the side seams, and the lining to the sides and across the hem if preferred.
6 With a vent, reinforce the seam where it ends, 10 cm, (4 in.) above the new back hemline.
7 Turn up the back hem, right sides together, and stitch at either end.
8 Trim and turn back to the wrong side. Catch stitch the hem and the lining back into position down the sides of the coat, and across the back hemline.
9 Re-stitch the lining to the side seams at the front of the coat, and re-stitch the hem.
10 On the right side of the coat, put a bar across the top of the vent at each side, either with a close zig-zag stitch or by hand, to strengthen the vent.

Alterations which help Access and Movement

Letting in panels to ease movement
(see Fig. 38a and 38b on p. 58)

1 Mark on the garment with chalk the area you wish to replace with knitted fabric.
2 Unpick the sleeve band and/or waistband that will be affected.
3 Trace off the shapes of the areas to be replaced on to paper and add seam allowances.
4 Cut away the parts to be replaced, leaving a seam allowance on each edge of the garment.
5 Re-stitch the seams adding the knitted panels, neaten the edges, and replace the sleeve bands and waistband.

Alterations to trousers for people with the use of only one hand (see Fig. 30 on p. 51)

1 Unpick the underlying end of the waistband.
2 Mark where it comes to on the back of the overlying section when the trousers are fastened.
3 Make a vertical buttonhole at this point which measures the width of the waistband, but is worked only on the inside fabric of the waistband.
4 Place some 2.5 cm, (1 in.) wide elastic around the waist to give a comfortable fit and cut 2.5 cm, (1 in.) longer.
5 Slot the elastic through the waistband and out through the new buttonhole.
6 Stitch the elastic into a continuous band.

Shortening a skirt front to give a good appearance

1 Tie a string around your natural waist and mark the position of the string.
2 Take the waistband off and cut away the excess fabric, leaving a 1.5 cm, ($\frac{5}{8}$ in.) seam allowance above the new waisline mark.
3 Replace the waistband.
The darts may need to be re-positioned on a straight skirt, but with an elasticated waistband this does not arise. Safety pins are useful for marking the new waistline because they do not fall out.

Drop-front trousers (Fig. 80)

1 To alter ready-made trousers, measure the amount of overlap on the waistband at the front before removing the waisband. (Tailored trousers have a two-piece waistband, jeans a one-piece waistband.)
2 Fasten the zip and stitch across the top of the trousers just above the waist seam (Fig. 80a).
3 Unpick the side seams to the seat line and insert a zip on each side.
4 If the waistband is in two pieces use the shorter piece to re-stitch to the front of the trousers (Fig. 80b).
5 Re-stitch the longer waistband to the back of the trousers, leaving an overlap at each side (Fig. 80b).
6 Re-stitch the front waistband at each end, and both waistbands on the inside (Fig 80b).
7 Fasten each side with hooks and bars, or buttons (Fig. 80c).
8 Place some 2.5 cm (1 in.) wide elastic around the waist to fit comfortably and add another 2.5 cm (1 in.) (Fig. 80c).
9 Slot the elastic through the back waistband and button together at the front. This will hold the back in position when the front is let down (Fig. 80c).

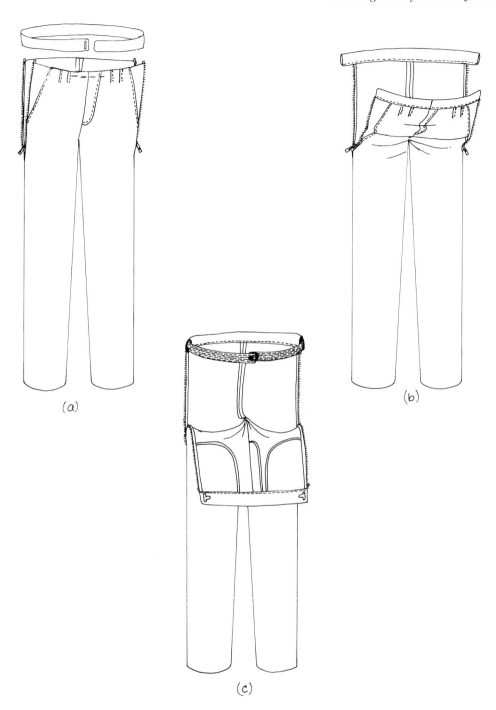

(a)

(b)

(c)

80 Drop front trouser alteration

10 CLOTHING WORKSHOPS AND THE FUTURE

The first workshop producing clothing for people with special needs was set up at Shipley, near Bradford, in December 1982. At this workshop garments are made on a one-off basis, in consultation with the clients, to ensure that their needs and wishes are met.

Over the years, similar workshops have been established in various locations in the United Kingdom. The majority have been funded by the Manpower Services Commission under the Community Programme scheme. This programme came to an end in 1988 and has been replaced by Employment Training. The majority of workshops have continued under this scheme, but the emphasis has moved from service provision to training and has had an effect on the quantity of garments produced. However, it is hoped that as each training programme becomes more firmly established there will be a subsequent improvement in service. The addresses of clothing workshops in the United Kingdom are listed below:

Address
Fashion Services for the Disabled
Greenfield Centre
Green Lane
Baildon
BRADFORD
BD17 5JS
Telephone: 0274 597487

Area of Operation and Service Offered
Bradford Metropolitan area. Full range of made-to-measure garments, home visits, workshop accessible to wheelchairs.

Disability Clothing Designs
Hatherlay Road Day Centre
Hatherlay Road
GLOUCESTER
Telephone: 0452 309461

No area restriction. Full range, etc. Home visits within a reasonable distance. Workshop accessible to wheelchairs.

Bassetlaw Fashion Services for the Disabled
Unit 7
Canalside Workshops
Leverton Road
RETFORD
Nottinghamshire
DN22 0DR
Telephone: 0777 860206

No area restriction. Full range, etc. Home visits within a 30-mile radius. Workshop accessible to wheelchairs.

Address

Spinning Jenny Ltd
Unit 29
Castleton Centre
York Road
BELFAST
BT15 3HR
Telephone: 0232 351370

The above workshops are funded by Local
Authorities or the voluntary sector. Those
following are operated under the Employment
Training Scheme:

Chapeltown & Harehills Resource Centre
161 Harehills Lane
LEEDS
LS8 3QE
Telephone: 0532 491087

CEDEMP Fashion Services for the Disabled
Southlands Centre
MIDDLESBROUGH
TS3 0HG
Telephone: 0642 327584

CEDEMP Fashion Services for the Disabled
89–95 Lord Street
REDCAR
Cleveland
TS10 3HR
Telephone: 0642 479948

Community Rural Aid Ltd
C/o Scandura Tapes
1 Manor Road
St Helens Auckland
BISHOP AUCKLAND
Telephone: 0388 608786

Wearside Disablement Centre Trust
46 & 47 Hutton Close
Crowther Estate
WASHINGTON
NE38 0AH
Telephone: 091 415 1964

Oakmill Services for the Disabled
Unit DI
Northbridge Centre
Elm Street
BURNLEY
BB10 1PD
Telephone: 0282 416711

Area of Operation and Service Offered

Northern Ireland area. Full range, etc.
Home visits undertaken.
Workshop accessible to wheelchairs.

Leeds area. Home visits undertaken.
Workshop accessible to wheelchairs.

No area restriction. Full range, etc.
Home visits within Cleveland.
Workshop accessible to wheelchairs.

No area restriction. Full range, etc.
Home visits within the Langtaurgh district.
Workshop accessible to wheelchairs.

No area restriction.
Home visits undertaken.
Workshop accessible to wheelchairs.

No area restriction.
Home visits within a 20-mile radius.
Workshop accessible to wheelchairs.

Area covers Burnley, Blackburn, Colne and
    East Lancashire. Full range, etc.
Home visits undertaken.
Workshop accessible to wheelchairs.

Address	Area of Operation and Service Offered
Spastics Society Tudor House Langshaw Lea Netherley LIVERPOOL L27 4YA *Telephone:* 051 488 0444	No area restriction. No home visits able to be undertaken. Workshop accessible to wheelchairs.
Wirral Fashion for the Disabled 1 Berner Street Birkenhead MERSEYSIDE L41 4AJ *Telephone:* 051 647 5373	No area restrictions. Limited home visits undertaken. Workshop accessible to wheelchairs.
North Peckham Sewing Workshop 257 Rye Lane Peckham LONDON SE15 *Telephone:* 01 252 8052	New project. Information available direct from workshop.
Fashion for the Disabled Work-Start Business Centre Logie Avenue DUNDEE Scotland DD2 2AR *Telephone:* 0382 67523	No area restriction. Full range, etc. Home visits undertaken within the Tayside area. Workshop accessible to wheelchairs.
Fashion for the Disabled 95 Carron Place Kelvin Industrial Estate East Kilbride Scotland *Telephone:* 03552 37541	Undergoing structural change. Information available direct from workshop.

The following organizations offer some services:

Address	Area of Operation and Service Offered
Age Concern Rotherham Ltd ROMAC House 49–53 St Ann's Road ROTHERHAM *Telephone:* 0709 829621	Rotherham area. Alteration and adaptation service for the elderly. Some disabled clients can be accepted.
Faichney Field Day Centre 96 Main Street East Kilbride Scotland *Telephone:* 03552 34986	Repairs and alterations for Day Centre members.

From the above list it will be quite apparent that large areas of the country are without provision of any kind. Some workshops are able to provide a mail order service and there are areas of disability where this can be helpful. However, if the major requirement is a correct and comfortable fit for someone of non-standard shape or proportion, a postal service may not offer a satisfactory solution and could become an expensive matter of trial and error.

For the present, an improvement in the number of operating workshops would be the best solution to ensure that everyone who needs special clothing can have that need met. In October 1988 a number of existing clothing workshops joined together to form the National Association of Clothing Workshops. One of the main aims of this Association is to promote an increase in provision for people with special clothing needs and to offer help and advice to anyone hoping to set up a workshop. The Association can be contacted via Fashion Services for the Disabled at Shipley.

The funding of workshops is a constant problem. If the aim is to provide a very specialized service to produce single, one-off garments for individual people then it has so far proved impossible to provide this kind of service on a commercial basis. There are various research programmes currently examining the feasibility of 3D computer pattern making. Such a system would be capable of transforming the whole of a complex body surface area into a flat printout pattern in one operation. This system would dispense with the most expensive element of made-to-measure garment production – that of measuring and pattern cutting. It is this aspect of the work which is labour-intensive and requires subsidies to allow people with disabilities to purchase garments at a price their able-bodied peers would expect to pay at any of the high street multiples. Such a computerized system is, however, some years away from being a marketable proposition.

At the present time Local Authority funding, business sponsorship, or other sources of finance are essential. All these bodies can be approached, but first of all it is as well to highlight a case which illustrates an unmet need. There may be a local survey detailing the numbers of people in that area with disabilities, and specific instances of individual difficulties could be cited. Established workshops also may be able to supply figures showing the number of customers they serve annually. The majority of workshops receive more orders than can be dealt with immediately and can have considerable waiting lists.

Having demonstrated that a need exists, it is as well to begin by lobbying the Local Authority. From then on, the local library can be valuable source of information. Discover the names and addresses of local MPs and, if possible, make an appointment to attend a surgery. Members of Parliament have no direct authority over how the Local Authority budget is spent, but they can be valuable allies once they are convinced that something should be done. Councillors vote to decide where money is spent. The local library reference section will have records of all council meetings, and from these it will be possible to discover which councillors sit on committees that have special responsibility for people with disabilities or for the elderly. Central libraries will have a copy of key personnel in all the metropolitan boroughs, county councils, London boroughs, district councils, and councils in Wales, Scotland and Ireland. In addition, it may be useful to contact local hospitals to get the backing of the occupational therapy and physiotherapy departments. Last, but not least, local branches of prominent disability charities should be approached and their support enlisted.

If all these approaches produce concern, understanding, support and sympathy, but no hard cash, then appeals must be made to the business community. Economic Development Units and the Council for

Voluntary Service can both offer invaluable help in putting together an information package and business plan to present to businesses. They will also provide information on which companies it would be best to approach.

Ten years ago very little was being done regarding clothing for disabled people. Able-bodied people now have a much greater awareness of the clothing problems created by disability and are keen to help, and people with a disability are realizing that the choice available to their able-bodied peers can be theirs. Self-help may well be the answer for the time being, but with a distinct change in people's attitudes and the advancement of computer design, the future looks distinctly rosy.

USEFUL ADDRESSES

Information and Advice

British Man-Made Fibres Federation,
24 Buckingham Gate
London
SW1E 6LB

Confederation of British Wool Textiles
60 Toller Lane
Bradford
BD8 9BZ

Courtaulds Fibres Ltd
Performance Products
P.O. Box 16
Foleshill Road
Coventry
CV6 5AE

Home Laundering Consultative Council
British Apparel Centre,
7 Swallow Place
London
W1R 7AA

ICI Fibres
Hookstone Road,
Harrogate
North Yorks
HG2 8QN

International Institute for Cotton
21 Cavendish Place
London
W1M 9DL

International Wool Secretariat
Development Centre
Valley Drive
Ilkley
Yorkshire
LS29 8PB

Specialist Products and Services

Carrington Sci-Tex
P.O. Box 10
Barrowford
Nelson
Lancashire
BB9 8NH
(Manufacturers and suppliers of
flame-retardant/resistant fabrics.)

Harlequin
E.A. & H.M. Bull Ltd
Unit 25
Jubilee End
Lawford
Manningtree
Essex
CO11 1UR
(Buttons, belts and buckles covered in
costomers fabric by post.)

J.V. Landers
Metropolitan Workshops
Enfield Road
London
N1 5AZ
(Machine pleating, covered buttons, picot
edging by post.)

Milner Leather
Unit 5
Corris Craft Centre
Machynlleth
Powys
SY20 9RF
(Leathers, tools, patterns and materials by
post.)

Panotex Universal Carbon Fibres Ltd
P.O. Box 2
Gomersal Mills
Cleckheaton
West Yorkshire
BD19 4LU
(Manufacturers and suppliers of
flame-retardant fabrics.)

Pennine Outdoor
Hard Knott
Holmbridge
Huddersfield
West Yorks
HD7 1NT
(Specialist outdoor fabrics and accessories,
waterproof and thermal, etc., by post.)

Tor Outdoor Pursuits
3 Fryer Street
Runcorn
Cheshire
WA7 1ND
(As Pennine Outdoor.)

General Fabric Suppliers (Mail Order)

J.W. Coates & Co. Ltd
Croft Mill
Lowther Lane
Foulridge
Colne
Lancashire
BB8 7NG

Fence End Fabrics
The Cottage
Fence End
Thornton-in-Craven
Nr Skipton
North Yorks
BD23 3JQ

MacCulloch & Wallis Ltd
25/26 Dering Street
London
W1R 0BH

60 Plus Textiles Ltd
Barley
Nelson
Lancashire
BB9 6LJ

USEFUL BOOKS

Colour, Line and Style

Bernat Klein, *An Eye for Colour*, Robin & Ruff (in print in America. Some libraries in the British Isles still have copies.)
Doris Pooser, *Always in Style*, Judy Piatkus (Publishers) Ltd.
Jane Procter, *Dress Your Best*, Guild Publishing, London.
Mary Quant and Felicity Green, *Colour by Quant*, Treasure Press.

Pattern Alterations and Sewing

Ann Ladbury, *The Batsford Book of Sewing*, BT Batsford Ltd.
Vogue Patterns, *The Vogue Sewing Book*, New York.

Adapting Patterns to Other Styles

Hilary Campbell, *Designing Patterns*, Stanley Thornes (Publishers) Ltd.
Winifred Aldrich, *Metric Pattern Cutting*, Mills and Boon.

INDEX